AUNT CAROLINE'S DIXIELAND RECIPES

A Rare Collection of Choice Southern Dishes

by
Emma McKinney

THE CONFEDERATE
REPRINT COMPANY
☆ ☆ ☆ ☆
WWW.CONFEDERATEREPRINT.COM

Aunt Caroline's Dixieland Recipes
by Emma McKinney

Originally Published in 1922
by Laird & Lee, Inc.
Chicago, Illinois

Reprint Edition © 2016
The Confederate Reprint Company
Post Office Box 2027
Toccoa, Georgia 30577
www.confederatereprint.com

Cover and Interior by
Magnolia Graphic Design
www.magnoliagraphicdesign.com

ISBN-13: 978-1945848087
ISBN-10: 1945848081

FOREWORD

In the art of cooking the "Old Southern Mammy" has few equals and recogonizes no peers.

The following recipes have, with great patience and kindly perseverance, been drawn from the treasured memories of Aunt Caroline Pickett, a famous old Virginia cook. The "pinch of this" and "just a smacker of that" so wonderfully and mysteriously combined by the culinary masters of the Southland have been carefully and scientifically amazed and recorded in this volume, and after a practical test of each recipe herein presented, the author can, with the fullest degree of confidence, recommend the following as the most attractive and economical combination ever presented.

The variety covers a range sufficient to fully gratify the demands of the modest as well as the exacting tastes of the most pronounced epicure, and have been carefully classified and alphabetically arranged for the convenience of the housewife. It is the author's intention that this little book become a veritable treasure trove of dainty, appetizing and tasty dishes.

In sweet memories of a happy childhood spent
in the atmosphere of the plantations and cabins
of Virginia under the benign influence of my
Dear Old Southern Mammy, Aunt Caroline,
this volume is affectionately dedicated.

CONTENTS

☆ ☆ ☆ ☆

Breads

Beverages

Cakes and Cookies

Candy

Meats

Pickles, Relishes

Pies and Desserts

Salads and Dressings

Contents 15

Soups

Vegetables

BREADS

☆ ☆ ☆ ☆

Virginia Beaten Biscuit

1 quart flour,
1 teaspoonful of salt,
1 tablespoon of lard.

Work lard lightly into the flour and salt, mix with iced water and then beat dough with rolling pin until it blisters. Cut into biscuits and bake in quick oven.

Southern Sweet-Potato Biscuits

2 cups flour,
1 cup of mashed boiled sweet potatoes,
2 tablespoonsful of lard,
1 teaspoonful of salt,
1 1/2 teaspoonfuls of baking powder,
1/2 teaspoonful of soda.

Enough buttermilk to make soft dough. Mix flour, salt, soda and baking powder together. Add sweet potatoes and work the lard in lightly. Mix with milk to make soft dough, roll thin, cut into biscuits and bake in quick oven.

Johnny Reb Cake

2 cupsful of flour,
1 cupful of yellow meal,
4 tablespoonsful of sugar,
1/2 teaspoonful of salt,
1 teaspoonful of Cream of Tartar,
1/2 teaspoonful of soda,
        or,
2 teaspoonsful of baking-powder.

Add enough milk or water to make a thin batter, and bake.

Spoon Bread

2 1/2 cups of fresh buttermilk,
1 scant half teaspoonful of soda mixed in with milk,
1 teaspoonful of salt,
3 tablespoonsful of meal,
3 eggs dropped in one at a time whole,
1 tablespoonful of lard (melted).

Mix in the order given and cook in baking dish in moderate oven.

Cinnamon Toast

Cut stale bread into thin slices, remove crusts, and cut in halves. Toast evenly, and spread first with butter, then with honey, and dust with cinnamon. Serve very hot.

Piedmont Corn Meal Mush

3 1/2 cups boiling water,
1 teaspoon salt,
1 cup fine corn meal.

Add meal to boiling salted water by sifting it slowly through the fingers, while stirring rapidly with the other hand. Boil for ten minutes, and cook over hot water for two hours. Serve hot as a cereal. Or pour into one-pound baking powder boxes to cool; fry in deep fat. Serve either for breakfast. or as an accompaniment to roast pork, or, with syrup, for dessert.

Virginia Corn Fritters

1 can corn,
1/2 cup milk,
1/2 cup dried and sifted crumbs,
1 teaspoon salt,
1 teaspoon baking powder,
1 egg well beaten,
1 tablespoon flour.

Chop the corn, and add other ingredients in order given. Drop from a tablespoon into hot, deep fat and fry until brown.

French Toast

1 egg slightly beaten,
1 tablespoon sugar,
1/4 teaspoonful salt,
3/4 cup milk or coffee,
4 slices bread.

Mix egg, salt, sugar, and liquid in a shallow dish. Soak bread in mixture, and cook on a hot greased griddle until brown, turning when half cooked. Serve plain or spread with jam.

Mammy's Graham Muffins

1 pint of Graham Flour,
1/2 cupful of molasses,
1/2 teaspoonful of salt,
1/2 pint of white flour,
1 teaspoonful of soda.

Put the salt into the flour and soda into the molasses, milk or water. Drop into muffin tins and bake twenty minutes.

Aunt Caroline's Corn Bread

3/4 cup corn meal,
3/4 cup flour,
3 teaspoonsful baking powder,
1 tablespoon sugar,
1/3 teaspoon salt,
1 beaten egg,
3/4 cup milk and water mixed,
2 tablespoons melted bacon fat.

Mix in order given, beat well, and bake in a well-greased shallow pan in a hot oven about twenty minutes. Half of the egg will make a very good corn bread. Left-over pieces may be split, lightly buttered, and browned in the oven.

Bolted Corn Meal Bread

2 cupsful of flour,
1 cupful of corn meal,
   (bolted is best)
2 cupsful of milk,
2 teaspoonsful of cream of tartar,
1 teaspoonsful of baking soda,
1 egg,
1/2 cupful of sugar,
1/2 teaspoonful of salt.

Stir the flour and meal together, adding cream of tartar, soda, salt and sugar. Beat the egg, add the milk to it, and stir into the other ingredients. Bake in a gem-pan twenty minutes.

Mammy's Light Rolls

Yeast,
1 egg beaten lightly,
1 tablespoonful of sugar,
1/2 cake of yeast, dissolved in 1/3 cup of cold water.
1 cup of hot potatoes mashed fine,
1 quart of flour,
1 tablespoonful of lard,
1 teaspoonful of salt.

Put yeast mixed in the order given in a bucket to rise. Let it rise for about forty-five minutes or longer. Then when risen, put it into the flour, which has been mixed with the salt and lard. Do not knead the flour, just stick it together and beat it for fifteen minutes with rolling pin. If yeast does not make dough soft enough a little warm water may be used. After beating the dough, put it into a vessel to rise in warm place for about three hours. When risen, roll it lightly until about one-fourth of an inch thick. Then cut with biscuit cutter and dip into hot grease. Lastly fold the biscuits over and put into pans to rise about an hour or more.

Graham rolls are made the same way.

Golden Toast

Toast as many slices of bread as desired. For twelve slices use three hard boiled eggs and about two cups of cream sauce. Mash the whites of the eggs fine and stir them into the cream sauce. Spread each piece of bread when toasted with cream sauce, and then grate yolks over the top. Return to oven and heat just before serving.

Mississippi Biscuits

2 cups of flour,
1/4 teaspoonful of soda,
1 1/2 teaspoonsful of baking powder,
1 teaspoonful of salt,
2 tablespoonfuls of lard.

Mix flour, baking powder and salt. Then work in lightly the lard and mix with sufficient milk to make soft dough. Roll thin, cut into biscuits with small biscuit cutter and bake in quick oven.

Virginia Waffles

1 1/2 cups of pastry flour,
2 teaspoonsful of baking powder,
1/2 teaspoonful of salt,
4 tablespoonsful of melted butter,
1 cup of milk,
2 eggs.

To beaten yolks add milk, flour, baking powder, salt and butter. Add stiffly beaten whites last.

Cotton Blossom Popovers

2 eggs,
1 cup of milk,
1 cup of flour,
1/2 teaspoonful of salt.

Beat eggs together, add milk, and salt and pour this on the flour. Mix well and bake about forty minutes in rather slow oven. Serve at once.

Dixie Biscuit

1 pint of milk,
1 teaspoonful of lard,
2 teaspoonsful of butter,
2 teaspoonsfuls of sugar,
1 heaping teaspoonful of salt,
1/2 yeast cake,
6 cupfuls of flour.

Put milk on stove in double boiler with butter, salt, lard and sugar. When milk becomes scalded, let it cool until blood heat. Dissolve yeast and stir it into the scalded milk. Then add to milk when cooled two and a half cups of flour and mix to a stiff batter. Next add an egg well beaten to the batter and put the batter in a warm place to rise. Let it rise bout five hours and then knead as for ordinary biscuit using three and a half cups of flour. Knead until dough can be handled easily, then roll out to one-half inch thickness. Rub each biscuit with melted butter, put two biscuits together and place in pans far enough apart not to touch. Bake fifteen or twenty minutes in hot oven.

Flour Muffins

2 eggs,
1 cup of milk,
1 1/2 cups of flour,
1 tablespoon of lard,
1 teaspoonful of salt,
2 teaspoonfuls of baking powder.

Beat eggs separately. To yolks, add salt, melted lard, milk, flour, and baking powder. Lastly, put in the well beaten whites and bake twenty or twenty-five minutes.

Baltimore Egg Bread

2 eggs,
3 cups of meal,
4 cups of sour milk,
1 tablespoonful of lard,
1 teaspoonsful of salt,
1/4 teaspoonful of soda,
1 1/2 teaspoonfuls of baking powder.

Beat eggs well together, add milk, meal, salt, soda and baking powder and lastly the hot melted lard. Bake in moderate oven. One cup of fresh corn cooked until tender may be added to the batter.

Southern Pastry

1 cup of flour,
1/4 teaspoonful of salt,
1/4 cup of lard or butter.

Mix flour and salt, work lard lightly into the flour and mix with iced water to make stiff dough. Do not knead dough at all, just mix lightly together.

Griddle Cakes

1 1/2 cups of stale bread crumbs,
2 cups of milk,
1 tablespoonful of butter,
1 teaspoonful of salt,
1/2 cupful of flour.

Scald milk and pour over bread crumbs. Beat two eggs well together, then add salt, milk and bread crumbs, flour and lastly the melted lard or butter.

Sally Lunn

1 quart of flour,
4 eggs,
1 tablespoonful of sugar,
1 cup of yeast,
1 cup of milk,
1 teaspoonful of salt,
1/2 cup of butter,
1/2 cup of lard.

Beat the eggs separately. Then mix and add yeast and sugar. Sift salt into flour, melt butter and lard and add eggs, yeast and milk before putting in flour. Leave in bowl and set away to rise. When risen, beat hard and put into greased pan to rise again. For seven o'clock tea make it at twelve.

Jeff Davis Muffins

2 eggs,
1 cup of sour milk,
1 cup of meal,
1/2 cup of flour,
1 teaspoonful of salt,
2 teaspoonsfuls of baking powder.
1 tablespoonful of lard.

Beat eggs separately. To yolks add salt, milk, melted lard, meal, flour and baking powder. Lastly put in the well beaten whites and bake in moderate oven.

Carolina Corn Meal Rolls

1 cup meal,
1 cup flour,
4 teaspoonsful baking powder,
1/2 teaspoon salt,
3 tablespoons bacon fat,
3/4 cup milk.

Mix and sift dry ingredients. Rub in shortening with finger tips. Add milk and mix thoroughly. Roll lightly on a floured board to a thickness of one-half inch. Cut with biscuit cutter, brush with milk or water, and fold double. Bake in hot oven fifteen minutes.

Carolina Brown Bread
(Baked)

1 cupful of Indian Meal,
1 cupful of rye meal,
1/2 cupful of flour,
1 cupful of molasses (scant),
1 cupful of milk or water,
1 teaspoonsful of soda.

Put the meals and flour together. Stir soda into molasses until it foams. Add salt and milk or water. Mix all together. Bake in a tin pail with cover on for two and a half hours.

Salt Rising Bread

Pour one pint of boiling sweet milk over three heaping tablespoonsful of corn meal. Beat well and set in a warm place all night. On the morning add to the mixture a pint of warm milk or water, a teaspoonful of sugar, and a pint of flour. Beat well and set in a warm place for about two hours or until it looks spongy. Then add one teaspoonful of salt, one tablespoonful of lard and enough flour to make a soft dough. Work fifteen minutes, knead into loaves, let them rise one or two hours, and then bake an hour or longer.

BEVERAGES

☆　　☆　　☆　　☆

Egg Nog – Maryland Style

Beat the yolk of one egg, add a teaspoonful of sugar, and a small pinch of salt, then pour in slowly stirring all the while a cup of milk. Pour in a glass and put spoonful of whipped cream on top and any quantity of "flavoring desired."

Swanee Fruit Punch

2 cups of sugar,
1 cup of water,
1 cup of tea,
1 pint of strawberry syrup,
Juice of 10 lemons,
Juice of 6 oranges,
2 cans of grated pineapple,
1 large bottle of Maraschino cherries.

Make syrup by boiling sugar and water together for ten minutes. Add the tea, fruit juices, pineapple, and strawberry syrup. Let stand thirty minutes, strain and add enough iced water to make one or one and one-half gallons of liquid. Turn into large punch bowl over a piece of ice and lastly add cherries. This quantity will serve about ten people.

Louisiana Coffee

One heaping tablespoonful of coffee, a little white of egg, one cup of boiling water (Allow this quantity for each person). Scald the coffee pot, add the coffee, egg, and sufficient cold water to moisten. Mix well, add the boiling water and cook five minutes. Then place where it will keep hot, but not cook, for fifteen minutes. It is then ready to serve.

Hot Chocolate

1 1/2 squares of baker's chocolate,
4 teaspoonsful of sugar,
Pinch of salt,
1 cup of boiling water,
3 cups of milk,
1/2 teaspoonful of vanilla.

Melt the chocolate over hot water. Add the sugar, salt and boiling water. When smooth, add the heated milk and cook twenty minutes in double boiler. Then beat with egg beater and flavor. More sugar may be added if desired.

An excellent substitute for whipped cream to serve with hot chocolate is marshmallows. Drop one in each cup of the hot liquid.

Tea – Southern Style

Take one-half teaspoonful of tea to one cup of boiling water. Put the tea in the pot, pour the boiling water upon it and let stand where it will keep hot for five minutes. Then serve. Tea should never be boiled for it makes it bitter.

Iced Tea

Use one scant teaspoonful of tea to one cup of boiling water. Pour boiling water over tea leaves and let stand until milk warm. Then strain and sweeten to taste while tea is still warm, as it requires less sugar. Serve with crushed ice, green mint leaves, and sliced lemon and orange.

Uncle Remus Mint Julep

3/4 cup sugar,
Juice 3 lemons,
1 cup of water,
4 sprigs of mints,
1 pint ginger ale,
            or
"Any flavoring desired."

Boil sugar and water ten minutes, and cool. Add strained lemon juice, mint leaves bruised, and ginger ale. Half fill glasses with crushed ice, and julep, and garnish with a sprig of mint.

Dewberry Vinegar

Over three quarts of dewberries pour one pint of vinegar and let it stand twenty-four hours. Strain and add one pound of sugar to one pint of juice. Scald twenty minutes and bottle tight. Strawberry and raspberry vinegar may be made in the same way.

CAKES AND COOKIES

Devil's Food Cake

2 eggs,
2 cups of brown sugar,
1 cup of butter,
1 cup of buttermilk,
3 cups of flour,
1/2 cake of melted chocolate,
1 1/2 tablespoons of cinnamon,
1 teaspoon of cloves,
1 teaspoon of allspice,
1 teaspoon of soda dissolved in 1/2 cup of boiling water.

Cream butter and sugar and add to well beaten eggs, next add milk, melted chocolate, flour beaten in lightly, vanilla and spices, and lastly the boiling water and soda. Bake in layer tins and moderate oven.

Filling For Devil's Food Cake

2 cups of white sugar,
1 cup of sweet milk,
1/2 cake of chocolate,
Yolk of 1 egg,
Butter size of an egg,
1 teaspoonful of Vanilla.

Put all the ingredients, except vanilla, on to cook. Cook until thick, then beat until creamy. Add vanilla and spread on layers.

Old Dominion Cake

Cream one cup of butter and two cups of powdered sugar. Add stiffly beaten whites of six eggs, three cups of flour, in which has been sifted two teaspoonsful of baking powder, and one teaspoonful of vanilla. Bake in layers in moderate oven.

Filling For Old Dominion Cake

Put on two cups of white sugar with enough water to dissolve thoroughly and cook until it spins a thread. Then add one teaspoonful of vanilla and pour slowly over the whites of two eggs beaten stiff. Beat until creamy and then spread on cake layers. Thickly strew the top of icing with raisins, English walnuts and blanched almonds.

Angel's Food Cake

Whites of 11 eggs,
1 cup of flour,
1 1/2 cups of sugar,
1 teaspoonful of cream of tartar,
1 teaspoonful of almond extract.

Sift flour and sugar together five times, then add cream of tartar. Have whites well beaten and add sugar and flour slowly, then almond extract. Beat very little after flour goes in and bake in round cake pan in moderate oven for about fifty minutes.

Filling

Put on to cook two and one-fourth cups of brown sugar, three tablespoonsful of cream, one tablespoonful of butter. Cook until thick, then beat until creamy and spread on layers.

Tutti Frutti Cake

2 cups of sugar,
1 cup of milk,
1 cup of butter,
3 cups of flour (sifted three times)
1 cup of cornstarch into which has been sifted 3 teaspoons of baking powder,
1 teaspoonful of almond extract.

Cream butter and sugar, add milk, flour, cornstarch and flavoring. Bake in layers in moderate oven.

Magnolia Sponge Cake

3 eggs beaten separately and then together,
1 1/2 cups of sugar,
1 1/2 cups of flour,
1 1/2 teaspoonsful of baking powder,
1/2 cup-of boiling water.

Mix in the order given and cook in biscuit pan in moderate oven.

Bride's Cake

Whites of 18 eggs,
1 pound of flour,
1 pound of sugar,
3/4 pound of butter.

Sift flour three times after adding to it a teaspoonful of soda, and two of cream of tartar. Cream butter and sugar until very light and add to the stiffly beaten whites. Next add the flour, beating it in lightly with the hand. Flavor with one teaspoonful of vanilla or almond extract and bake in slow oven.

Ponciania Cake

1 pound of butter,
1 pound of sugar,
1 pound of flour,
Juice and rind of 1 lemon,
9 eggs,
1 1/4 pounds of almonds (in shell),
1/2 pounds of citron,
1/2 pound of raisins.

Cream butter and sugar and add to well beaten yolks. Next add alternately the flour and the whites beaten stiff, then the fruits, which have been cut fine and dredged with flour, and lastly the nuts. Bake in a slow oven.

Sally White Cake

1 pound of butter,
1 pound of flour,
1 1/2 pounds of sugar,
1 dozen eggs,
3 pounds of citron chopped fine,
2 small cocoanuts (grated),
2 pounds of almonds (blanched and chopped fine),
1 wine glass of brandy,
1 wine glass of wine,
3 teaspoonsful of nutmeg,
2 teaspoonsful of mace.

Cream butter and sugar and add to well beaten yolks. Next add flour and whites beaten stiff, the fruit, nuts, brandy, wine and spices. Bake in slow oven from four to five hours.

Cabin Cake

To whites of eight eggs beaten stiff, add one cup of butter and two cups of sugar creamed together. Next add three-fourths cup of milk, three cups of flour, two teaspoonsful of baking powder and one teaspoonful of vanilla. Bake in layers in moderate oven.

Filling For Cabin Cake

Put on to cook two cups of sugar and half a cup of water. Boil without stirring until it jellies when dropped into cold water. Then pour over stiffly beaten whites of three eggs, stir into icing a small quantity of citron, currants, dates, figs, raisins, almonds, English walnuts (all chopped fine) and grated cocoanut, leaving out a similar quantity to be put on top of cake when iced.

Pride of Kentucky Cake

4 eggs,
3 cups of flour,
2 cups of sugar,
1 cup of butter,
1 cup of milk,
2 teaspoonsful of baking powder,
1 teaspoonful of vanilla.

Separate eggs leaving out two whites for filling. To beaten yolks, add butter and sugar creamed together, then the milk, flour, baking powder and vanilla and lastly whites of two eggs beaten stiff. Bake in layers in moderate oven, and put together with any kind of filling desired.

Gold and White Anniversary Cake

Whites of 8 eggs,
2 cups of sugar,
1 cup of crisco,
3 cups of flour,
1 cup of milk,
2 teaspoons of baking powder.
1 teaspoon of vanilla.

Cream crisco and sugar and add to stiffly beaten whites, then add the milk. Next beat the flour in lightly, and add baking powder and vanilla. Bake in layer cake tins in a moderate oven.

Filling for Anniversary Cake

Yolks of 6 eggs,
3 cups of sugar,
Enough water to dissolve sugar thoroughly.

Put sugar and water on to cook. Let it cook until it spins a thread, then gradually pour it over the yellows, which have been beaten until thick. Beat until filling becomes creamy, add one teaspoonful of vanilla, and spread on layers.

Marguerites

Whites of three eggs beaten stiff. Add three tablespoonsful of sugar slowly. Put on top of butter-thins and sprinkle over with ground nuts and brown in oven.

Pickaninny Cookies

Sift one quart of flour, make a hole in the center, put in two cups of sugar, one of lard, one beaten egg, and one cup of sweet milk, into which has been stirred a half teaspoonful of soda. Work all together, roll thin and bake in a quick oven.

Apple Sauce Cake

1 cup of butter,
1 cup of brown sugar,
1 cup of apple sauce,
1 1/2 teaspoonsful of soda (mixed in with apple sauce),
2 cups of flour,
1 cup of raisins,
1 cup of currants,
2 eggs.

Betsy Ross Pound Cake

1 pound of flour,
3/4 pound of butter,
1 pound of sugar,
12 eggs.

Cream butter and about two-thirds of the flour together. Beat whites of eggs to a stiff froth, beat yolks of eggs and sugar together until very light. Mix thoroughly all the ingredients, stirring in last the loose flour. Bake in a slow oven until done.

Marshmallow Filling

1/4 pound of marshmallows,
Whites of 2 eggs,
1 cup of sugar,
1/2 cup of water.

Boil sugar and water until it spins a thread. Cut up marshmallows and pour boiling water over them to steam. When sugar is done, pour gradually over the whites of two eggs beaten stiff, then add marshmallows. Beat until creamy and spread on cake layers.

Martha Washington Cake

4 eggs,
2 cups of sugar,
1 cup of butter,
1 cup of sweet milk,
3 cups of flour,
1 teaspoonful of baking powder,
1/2 pound of raisins,
1 teaspoonful each of cinnamon, cloves and all-spice.

Cream butter and sugar and add to well beaten eggs. Next add the milk, flour, baking powder, raisins and spices. Bake in layers in moderate oven.

Filling For Martha Washington Cake

2 cups of sugar,
Juice and grated rind of 2 lemons,
2 cups of grated cocoanut,
1 cup of boiling water.

When this begins to boil, add one tablespoonful of cornstarch dissolved in a little cold water. Cook until it spins a thread, then beat until creamy and spread between layers.

Chocolate Sauce

1 tablespoonful of butter,
1 cupful of sugar,
2 tablespoonsful of cocoa,
4 tablespoonsful of boiling water.

Put the butter into an agate dish on the stove; when melted, stir in the cocoa and sugar dry. Add boiling water and stir until smooth. Add vanilla to taste.

Virginia Doughnuts

2 eggs beaten light,
2 cups of sugar,
3 level tablespoonsful of melted butter,
1 cup of sour milk (if sweet milk is used, add 1 teaspoonful of cream of tartar),
4 cups of flour,
1/2 teaspoonful of soda,
1/2 teaspoonful of cinnamon,
1/2 teaspoonful of salt.

Mix in the order given, adding the dry ingredients sifted together and enough more flour to make a dough just soft enough to handle. Have the board well-floured, and the fat for frying and heating. Roll out only a little at a time, cut into rings with an open cutter. Do all the cutting before frying, as that will take your entire attention. The fat should be hot enough for the dough to rise to the top instantly.

Plantation Cookies

2 eggs,
1 cupful of sugar,
1 1/2 cupfuls of oatmeal, or rolled oats,
2/3 cupful of cocoanut,
1/4 teaspoonful of salt,
1/2 teaspoonful of vanilla,
2 tablespoonsful of butter.

Cream the butter and sugar together and add the well-beaten eggs. Add the remainder of the ingredients and drop on a well greased baking-pan. Bake in a moderate oven from fifteen to twenty minutes.

Jelly Roll Cake

4 eggs,
1 cupful of sugar,
1 cupful of flour,
1 teaspoonful of cream of tartar,
1/2 teaspoonful of soda,
Pinch of salt,
1 teaspoonful of extract of lemon.

Beat together eggs and sugar, add salt and extract. Stir into the dry flour the soda and cream of tartar. Mix all together. Bake in a moderate oven, in a large pan, and turn out, when done, on a clean towel, which has been sprinkled with powdered sugar. Spread with jelly and roll while warm.

Aunt Sug's Nut Cookies

1 1/2 cups of sugar,
1 cup of crisco or butter,
3 eggs,
1 tablespoonful of cinnamon,
1/2 teaspoonful of salt,
1 teaspoonful of soda, dissolved in 4 tablespoonful of hot water,
3 cups of flour,
1 cup each of raisins, currants, and English walnuts or almonds broken up.

To well-beaten eggs add creamed butter and sugar, cinnamon, soda, water, flour, fruits, which must be dredged with flour, and nuts. Lastly add one teaspoonful of vanilla and drop by spoonful into greased pans. Bake in moderate oven.

Ginger Snaps

1/2 cup of brown sugar,
1 cup of molasses,
1/2 cup of butter,
1 teaspoonful of baking powder,
1 teaspoonful of ginger,
1/2 pint of flour to begin with.

Put butter, powder and sugar into flour, add ginger and molasses. Add more flour if needed. Roll out thin and bake in a quick oven.

Mason and Dixon Cookies

1 cup of brown sugar,
1/2 cup of melted shortening,
1 egg,
1/2 cup of sweet milk,
1/2 teaspoonful of soda sifted with flour,
1 1/2 cups of flour,
1/2 cup of chopped raisins,
1/2 cup of chopped nuts,
1/2 teaspoonful of salt,
3 squares of melted chocolate.

Mix in order given and bake in moderate oven.

Fruit Cake

1 pound of white sugar,
3/4 pound of butter,
1 pound of flour (1 quart) sifted.
2 pounds of raisins,
1 pound of currants,
1 pound of dates,
1/2 pound of citron,
10 eggs,
1 pound of figs,
1 ounce each of cinnamon, nutmeg and cloves,
2 teaspoonsful of baking powder mixed in with
flour,
1 wine glass of brandy and one of wine.

Cream butter and sugar and add to well beaten yolks. Then add alternately the flour and whites of the eggs beaten stiff; then the wine and brandy spices. Lastly add the fruit which has been chopped fine and dredged with flour, mix well together and bake about four hours in a slow oven.

CANDY

☆　　☆　　☆　　☆

U.D.C. Cocoanut Candy

2 cups of white sugar,
1/2 cup of milk,
1 cup of grated cocoanut,
1 teaspoonful of vanilla,
Butter the size of an egg.

Put sugar, milk and butter on to cook. Let it cook until it will form a soft ball when tried in cold water. Add vanilla, remove from stove, and beat in the cocoanut until it becomes creamy. Pour into buttered plates and cut into squares when cold.

Mexican Kisses

3 cups of white sugar,
1 cup of milk,
Butter the size of an egg,
1 cup of nuts,
1 teaspoonful of vanilla.

Put sugar and butter and milk on to cook. Cook until it will form a soft ball when tried in cold water. Add vanilla, remove from stove and beat until creamy. Then put in nuts and drop from spoon on buttered papers.

Mammy's Peanut Candy

2 cups of brown sugar,
1 cup of chopped peanuts,
1 cup of water,
Butter the size of an egg.

Cook about twenty minutes, beat until creamy, and pour into buttered plates. When cold cut into squares.

Divinity Candy

3 cups of white sugar,
3/4 cup of white Karo syrup,
Whites of 2 eggs,
3/4 cup of water,
1 teaspoonful of vanilla.

Put sugar, syrup and water on to cook. Let it cook until it will form a hard ball when tried in cold water. Remove from stove and pour gradually over stiffly beaten whites. Add vanilla and one cup of nuts and beat until creamy. Pour into buttered plates and cut into squares when cold.

Almonds, Creamed

Shell and blanch burnt almonds and lay them in the open oven to dry, but do not let them brown. Put one cup of granulated sugar over the fire with a tablespoon of water; stir until it is well dissolved and comes to a boil. Drop into this the blanched almonds a few at the time and take them out immediately with a perforated spoon or candy dipper, laying them on waxed paper until they harden, or upon buttered plates.

Chocolate Caramels

Mix in a saucepan two cups of brown sugar, half a cup each of molasses (not syrup) and cream, half a cake of unsweetened chocolate, and four tablespoons of butter, bring to a boil slowly, taking care the sugar does not scorch before it is entirely melted. Cook steadily until a little of the candy is brittle if dropped in cold water, add two teaspoons vanilla, turn into a greased pan, and cut into squares as soon as it is cool.

Old Virginia Molasses Taffy

Put a pint of New Orleans molasses over the fire in a saucepan and boil for twenty minutes. Stir in a quarter teaspoon of baking soda and boil fifteen minutes longer, or until a little, dropped into cold water, becomes brittle. This candy must be stirred constantly while it is cooking or it will scorch. When it reaches the brittle stage, add a teaspoon of vinegar and a tablespoon of butter and pour into well-buttered pans. Mark into shape with a buttered knife after the candy begins to form and before it is really hard.

Cream Peppermint Drops

Put a half cup of cold water and two cups of granulated sugar into a clean saucepan and boil slowly, without stirring, until it spins thread from the tip of a spoon dipped into it. Take from the stove, leave it untouched until it is about blood-warm, then stir steadily, always in one direction until the mixture begins to become creamy. Flavor to taste with essence of peppermint, adding this cautiously so as not to get the flavor too strong. Drop by the teaspoonful upon waxed paper, being careful not to put the drops so close together that they will run into each other. A candy dipper is even better for this purpose than a teaspoon.

After Dinner Mints

2 cups of sugar,
1/3 cup boiling water,
1/4 cup molasses,
4 drops oil of spearmint.

Put sugar and molasses into a smooth, clean saucepan, and add boiling water, heat gradually to the boiling point, and boil to 258 degrees F., or until candy becomes brittle when tested in cold water, add flavoring, pour on an oiled slab or platter and when cool enough to handle pull until nearly white. Pull into long strips about half an inch in diameter, and cut in small pieces with scissors. Roll in powdered sugar, and keep in a covered jar for several days before using.

Peanut Butter Fudge

3 cups of white sugar,
3/4 cup of milk,
1/2 cup of peanut butter,
1 teaspoonful of vanilla.

Put sugar, peanut butter and milk on to cook. Let it cook until it will form a soft ball when tried in cold water. Add vanilla, remove from stove and beat until creamy. Pour into buttered plates and cut into squares when cold.

Chocolate Fudge

3 cups of brown sugar,
3/4 cup of water,
Butter the size of an egg,
1/2 cake of chocolate,
1 teaspoonful of vanilla.

Put sugar and water on to cook. When it begins to boil, add butter, and let it cook until it will form a soft ball when tried in cold water. Add vanilla, remove from stove, and beat in the chocolate. Beat until creamy, then pour into buttered plates. Cut into squares when cold.

Sea-Foam Candy

4 cups of brown sugar,
1 cup of water,
Whites of 2 eggs,
1 cup of nuts,
1 teaspoonful of vanilla.

Put sugar and water on to cook. Let it cook until it spins a thread. Then add vanilla, remove from stove, and pour slowly into whites of eggs beaten stiff. Beat until stiff and then drop from spoon on buttered paper. Add nuts just before candy gets creamy and hard.

MEATS

☆　　☆　　☆　　☆

Fried Chicken – Virginia Style

Cut a young tender dressed fowl into small pieces. Salt well and let stand several hours. Then wash and drain, dip each piece of chicken into flour, to which has been added salt and black pepper, and fry to a golden brown in deep hot fat. Let chicken fry slowly.

Creole Veal Patties

1 1/2 cupsful of boiled rice,
1 cupful of veal,
1/2 teaspoonful of salt,
1/2 teaspoonful of poultry dressing,
1 egg,
1 tablespoonful of milk.

Grind or chop the veal, salt, and stir into the rice with the dressing; beat the eggs, add milk, and stir all together. Drop a tablespoonful spread out thin on the griddle, and fry as you would griddle-cakes. Pork, or lamb may be used instead of veal.

Sugar Cured Ham Loaf

1 pound raw ham,
2 beaten eggs,
1 cup dried crumbs,
1/2 teaspoon mustard,
1 cup boiling water,
1/4 teaspoon salt.

Put ham, including the fat, through meat chopper. Add crumbs, water, eggs, and seasoning. Mix well, and bake in a small bread pan, in a slow oven, an hour and a half; or cook in steamer two hours.

Baked Rice and Ham

1/2 cup rice,
1 tablespoon onion finely chopped,
2 1/2 cups stock or water,
2 cups milk,
2 tablespoonsful carrot finely chopped,
1/2 cup cooked ham finely chopped.

Wash rice, place in greased baking dish; and liquid, ham, vegetables, and salt if necessary. Bake slowly for three hours, stirring occasionally during the first hour. Ham stock or corned beef stock may be used, and any cooked meat substituted for ham. Serve with boiled spinach or dressed lettuce.

Martha Washington Cheese Pudding

Slice one-half pound of cheese in thin slices, cover with water and cook on top of the stove until cheese has thoroughly melted. Then remove from the stove and when cool add to it two eggs well beaten, one tablespoon of flour, one-half teaspoon of salt, pinch of red pepper and one-fourth teaspoon of baking powder. Put in greased baking dish, cover top with bits of butter and bake in moderate oven.

Uncle Remus Omelette

To four eggs beaten separately add three table-spoonfuls of milk, a small quantity of butter and a pinch of salt. Pour quickly into a hot greased pan. Let remain on stove two minutes, then place inside oven for three minutes. Take out and fold twice. Serve immediately.

Old Fashioned Mince Meat

4 cupfuls of chopped meat,
12 cupfuls of chopped apples,
2 cupfuls of chopped suet,
1 cupful of vinegar,
3 cupfuls seeded raisins,
1 cupful seeded currants,
5 cupfuls of brown sugar,
1 1/2 cupfuls of molasses,
6 teaspoonsful of cinnamon,
3 teaspoonsful of cloves,

1 teaspoonful of nutmeg,
1/2 pound of citron,
Rind and juice of one lemon,
Butter the size of an egg,
Salt.

Moisten with cold coffee or strong tea. Cook slowly two hours.

Fish Balls a la Maryland

1 cupful of hot mashed potatoes,
1/2 cupful of shredded cod-fish,
2 teaspoonsful of melted butter,
2 tablespoonsful of milk,
Salt to taste.

Put the fish into a piece of cheese-cloth, let cold water run over it, and squeeze dry. Mix ingredients all together. Take a little flour in the hand and roll half a tablespoonful of the mixture between the palms, to the size of a small peach. Fry in deep fat.

Liver Fricasee

1 pound liver,
4 tablespoons flour,
2 cups boiling water,
3/4 teaspoon salt,
2 tablespoons bacon fat,
1/4 teaspoon paprika,

1 tablespoon grated onion,
6 slices toast.

Cut liver into half-inch cubes, and soak in cold salted water fifteen minutes. Drain. Cover with the boiling water, and simmer six minutes. Cook bacon fat, onion and flour until brown. Add seasonings, and stock in which liver was cooked. Stir until smooth. Add liver, and pour over toast or small, thin baking powder biscuit.

Breaded Pork Chops, Philadelphia Style

6 chops,
1 egg,
1/2 cupful of milk,
1 cupful of bread crumbs,
Pinch of salt.

Beat the egg and milk together, adding the salt. Dip the chops into this mixture, then into the crumbs. Fry in hot fat. Veal cutlets can be served in the same way.

Salmon Croquettes

One can of salmon, the yolks of six hard boiled eggs. Mix and season to taste with salt and pepper. Beat into the mixture one raw egg. Add three or four grated crackers and brown in hot lard.

Creamed Oysters

1 pint small oysters,
Milk,
2 1/2 tablespoons butter,
1/4 teaspoon paprika,
1/3 teaspoon celery salt.

Cook oysters in their own liquor until plump. Drain and measure the liquor. Melt butter, add flour, and blend well. Add oyster liquor, and enough milk to make two cups. Stir until smooth, add seasonings and oysters, and serve on toast. Garnish with toast points and sliced pickles.

Deviled Crabs

1 pint of crab meat,
2 hard boiled eggs,
2 tablespoonsful melted butter,
3 tablespoonsful vinegar, pepper, salt, and mustard to taste,
1 raw egg, well beaten.

Drain the liquor from the crabs, cream the yolks of the eggs with the butter, add seasoning, then stir in the raw egg, then the chopped whites of the eggs and mix well with the crab meat. Wash the shells and fill them lightly. Put grated bread crumbs over the top and pour over each two tablespoonsful of melted butter. Place in pan and bake until light brown.

Aunt Caroline's Beef Loaf

Two pounds of beef ground in a meat chopper. Add to this one-half cup of grated bread crumbs, two beaten eggs, a little onion, salt and pepper to taste. Roll into a loaf, cover the top with bits of butter and cook in oven for one and one-half hours. The juice of a can of tomatoes poured over the loaf while baking gives a delicious flavor.

Mammy's Chicken Patties

1 cup of cold diced chicken,
2 tablespoons of flour,
1/2 teaspoon of salt, cayenne pepper to taste,
1 cup of chicken stock.

Melt butter in sauce pan. Stir in flour, add chicken stock, season and bring to boiling point. Add chicken and cook slowly for five minutes. Fill patty shells and serve at once.

Baked Fish

Clean, rinse and wipe dry a white fish or any fish weighing three or four pounds. Rub the fish inside and out with salt and pepper, fill with a stuffing like that for poultry, but drier. Put in a hot greased pan, dredge with flour and cover the top with bits of butter. Bake an hour and a half.

Carolina Broiled Steak

Sprinkle the bottom of a skillet generously with salt. Place on the fire and let it become quite hot. Then put in the steak, turning often so as to retain the juice. When done place on a heated platter and season with pepper and bits of butter.

Deviled Eggs

Cut hard boiled eggs in two the long way. Remove the yolks and mash very fine. Add vinegar, sugar, salt, pepper and mustard to taste, also a little butter, mix well, put back into the whites and serve on lettuce leaves or garnished with parsley. For a change, ground olives, chicken or boiled ham may be used with the yolks.

Massa's Cheese Croquettes

3 tablespoonsful shortening,
1/4 teaspoon paprika,
1/3 cup bread flour,
1/4 teaspoon mustard,
1 cup hot milk,
Few grains cayenne,
1/4 teaspoon salt,
1 cup cheese cut fine.

Melt shortening, add flour; add hot milk, and stir until smooth and thick. Add seasonings and cheese, and pour into a shallow dish to cool. Shape into small pyramids, roll in sifted crumbs, dip in egg, and again in crumbs, and fry in deep fat until brown. Serve immediately.

Oysters With Macaroni

Arrange two cups of cooked macaroni and one pint of small oysters in layers in a buttered baking dish. Season each layer with salt and pepper, and dredge with flour. Cover with buttered crumbs and bake in a hot oven twenty minutes. One-fourth cup of grated cheese may be added.

Scalloped Oysters

1 quart of oysters,
1/4 pound of butter,
1/2 pound of cracker dust,
1/2 cup of rich cream,
Salt and pepper to taste.

Strew cracker dust and bits of butter over the bottom of an earthenware pan, then a layer of oysters. Proceed in this way until pan is filled, using a top layer of cracker dust and bits of butter. Add cream and bake about twenty minutes in a quick oven.

Creamed Dried Beef With Cheese

1/4 pound dried beef,
1 cup milk,
1 1/2 tablespoons butter,

2 tablespoons grated cheese,
2 tablespoons flour,
2 tablespoons ketchup.

Cut beef in small pieces, cover with boiling water, let stand five minutes and drain. Melt butter, add beef and stir until hot. Add flour and milk and stir until smooth. Add cheese and ketchup, and stir until cheese is melted. Serve with baked potatoes.

Cheese Straws

1 cup of grated cheese,
1 cup of sifted flour,
1 tablespoonful of butter,
1 teaspoonful of salt,
1/4 teaspoonful of cayenne pepper,
1/4 teaspoonful of baking powder.

Mix flour, cheese, salt, butter, pepper and baking powder. Mix with iced water to make stiff dough. Cut in long slender strips. Place in greased pans and bake in quick oven.

Chicken a la King

Boil a chicken until tender and when cool cut in dice. To diced chicken add strips of pimentos and green peppers and a can of mushrooms. Season with salt and pepper and mix with cream sauce. Serve hot on buttered squares of toast.

Southern Hash

4 raw potatoes,
3/4 cup of water,
2 green peppers,
1 1/2 cups cold chopped beef,
2 tomatoes,
Salt and pepper,
1 onion,
Toast points.

Put vegetables through the meat chopper, using coarse cutter. Cook in the stock, covered, until tender. Add beef, salt, and pepper, and when hot turn on a platter and garnish with toast points. If corned beef and stock are used, use salt with care.

Mammy's Veal Loaf

Mix well together three pounds of finely chopped veal, with one-half pound pork. Add to this one-half cup of grated bread crumbs, two beaten eggs, a little onion, salt and pepper to taste. Roll into a loaf and pour the juice of a can of tomatoes over the loaf and two tablespoonsful of butter. Cook in oven for one hour and half.

Chicken Croquettes

Boil chicken until tender, then chop very fine. Season with a little parsley chopped fine, salt and red and black pepper to taste. Mix with cream sauce and shape into croquettes. Roll croquettes in beaten egg, then in bread crumbs and fry in deep hot fat.

Cream Sauce

Put two cups of milk on stove to scald. Into two tablespoonsfuls of melted butter rub two tablespoonsful of flour until smooth. Then add scalded milk a little at the time to prevent lumping and season with salt and pepper. Stir constantly until thick, then remove from the stove.

Perlean

Dress and cut up one chicken as for frying. Boil until very tender, then add two cups of rice, half a cup of butter, some salt and plenty of pepper. Cook until it can be eaten with a fork.

PICKLES AND RELISHES

☆　☆　☆　☆

Aunt Caroline's Own Pickle

Chop fine one-half gallon of green tomatoes, one pint of onions, one pint of green and red peppers with seeds taken out, and one gallon of cabbage. Mix well and sprinkle two tablespoonsful of salt over it and let stand all night. Add three quarts of vinegar, two pounds of sugar, three teaspoonsful of celery seed, three of mustard seed two of spice, and one of cloves. Let simmer two hours.

Tar Heel Chow Chow

Chop one head of cabbage, one gallon of green tomatoes, and one quart of onions. Add one-half cup of salt, put in a bag and let it drain for twenty-four hours.

Then put in kettle and add about two pounds of brown sugar, one cup of white mustard seed, and one-half cup of celery seed. Cover with good apple vinegar and cook until done, about three or four hours. To the above add one or two pods of chopped red pepper.

Georgia Watermelon Rind Pickle

Cut rinds and soak over night in water to which has been added one cup of lime to a gallon of water. Rinse in four full waters and boil until tender in tea made of one-half gallon of water and four tablespoonsful of ginger. Then cook in the following syrup:

4 pounds of sugar,
1 quart of vinegar,
2 tablespoonsful of ground cinnamon,
1 tablespoonful of allspice,
2 tablespoonsful of whole cloves.
Cook until syrup is thick.

Apple Relish

7 pounds of apples,
2 pounds of seeded raisins,
1 pint of vinegar,
3 1/2 pounds of sugar,
2 oranges,
1 teaspoonful of powdered cloves,
2 teaspoonsful of powdered cinnamon.

Chop the raisins and put them into a porcelain lined kettle, add the apples, chopped and unpeeled, the juice and the chopped peel of the oranges, the sugar, vinegar and spices. Boil steadily for half an hour.

Corn Relish

18 ears of corn,
1 onion,
1 cabbage,
1/4 pound of mustard,
1 pint of vinegar,
4 cupsful of sugar,
1/2 cupful of salt,
2 peppers.

Cut the corn from the cob, chop, onion, peppers and cabbage, add sugar, salt and vinegar, and cook slowly three-quarters of an hour. Ten minutes before taking from the fire, add a very scant fourth of a pound of dissolved mustard. Seal in glass jars.

Bell Pepper Relish

1 dozen green peppers,
12 red peppers,
6 medium sized onions,
1 quart of vinegar,
1 1/2 cupsful of sugar,
2 tablespoonsful of salt.

Cut the peppers and onions into small pieces, sprinkle with salt and cover with boiling water. Let stand until cool, then drain. Place in a kettle, and add the vinegar, and sugar. Cook for twenty minutes. Put into jars, seal and set away until needed. Serve with cold meats.

Green Tomato Pickle

2 quarts of green tomatoes,
6 large onions,
3 red peppers,
4 quarts of cabbage, all chopped fine,
2 ounces of white mustard seed,
1/2 ounce of celery seeds,
2 1/2 pounds of sugar,
1/2 ounce of tumeric,
1 gill of salt,
2 quarts of vinegar.

Soak tomatoes, onions and cabbage in salt water one half hour, wash and drain. Add other ingredients and boil twenty minutes.

Cucumber Pickle

Take enough cucumbers to fill a two-gallon jar. Cut into lengthwise pieces and soak until fresh. Cover with equal parts of water and vinegar, and boil an hour and ten minutes. Then take them out and boil one and one-half hours in one gallon of fresh vinegar, two pounds of sugar, one tablespoonful of celery seed, one tablespoonful of tumeric, one teaspoonful each of cloves, mace and ginger, one tablespoonful of black pepper, and one of horse radish. When cold add one-half teaspoonful of cayenne pepper.

Piccalli

1/2 peck of ripe tomatoes,
1/2 peck of green tomatoes,
1 dozen sweet peppers, half of them green and half ripe or red,
11 small onions,
2 quarts of vinegar,
1 quart of brown sugar,
1 tablespoonful each of all kinds of spices.

Grind in coarse meat chopper, cover with one cup of salt and let stand over night. Next morning squeeze and put on to cook with sugar, vinegar and spices. Cook about half an hour or longer.

Stuffed Peppers

Wash as many fresh green peppers as desired. Then remove the tops from the peppers, scoop out the seeds, and fill with grated ham mixed with cream sauce. Cover with bread crumbs and bits of butter and bake until ready in a hot oven.

Peach Pickle

Peel peaches and put in stone jar. To seven pounds of fruit, use three and one-half pounds of sugar and one quart of vinegar. Boil sugar and vinegar together awhile and pour over fruit and flavoring, cinnamon, spice, ginger, cloves, nutmeg and mace may be used. Put in little sacks. Do this for seven or eight mornings.

Chili Sauce

1 dozen ripe tomatoes,
4 ripe or 3 green peppers,
2 tablespoonsful of salt,
2 tablespoonsful of sugar,
1 tablespoonful of cinnamon,
3 cups of vinegar.

Peel tomatoes and onions, chop very fine, add chopped peppers, and the other ingredients and boil one and one-half hours.

Mount Vernon Pickle

1 peck of green peppers,
1 string 6 inches long of red peppers,
1 large cabbage or 2 small ones,
4 large onions,
4 tablespoonsful of celery seed,
1/4 pound of black and white mustard seeds each,
2 tablespoonsful of tumeric.

Chop peppers, onions and cabbage fine and soak in one and a half cups of salt all night. Then cover well with vinegar and put equal parts of sugar. Add seasoning and cook about two and one-half hours.

English Chopped Pickle

1 large head of cabbage,
1 gallon of green tomatoes,
1 small bottle of sliced cucumber pickle (store pickle),
15 large onions.

Chop all fine and let stand over night, sprinkling them with salt. Do not put cabbage with onions and tomatoes. Next morning squeeze out the cabbage, onions and tomatoes, and put on in kettle. Add three quarts of vinegar, four pounds of brown sugar, one package of seedless raisins, one-half ounce of ground red pepper, eight tablespoonsful of white mustard seed, four tablespoonsful each of celery seed, one tablespoonful each of allspice, ginger, cloves and turmeric. Mix well together and cook about one hour.

PIES AND DESSERTS

Chess Pies

3 eggs,
2/3 cup of sugar,
1/2 cup of butter,
1/2 cup of milk.

Cream butter and sugar and add to the well beaten yolks. Then add milk and one teaspoonful of vanilla. Mix well and bake on a nice crust. When done, spread with the whites and three tablespoonful of sugar and a little flavoring. Return to oven and brown.

Heavenly Hash

Sweeten, flavor and whip stiff one pint of cream. Add to cream one-half pound of marshmallows cut into small pieces. Set on ice to chill. Then add one-half pound of blanched almonds chopped fine and garnish with maraschino cherries. Line bowl in which cream is put after being whipped, with powdered lady fingers or macaroons.

Food for the Gods

1 cup of sugar,
1/4 pound of dates,
1/4 pound of nuts,
3 tablespoonsful of cracker crumbs.

Beat whites of three eggs stiff and a one heaping teaspoonful of baking powder and the above ingredients. Cut the dates and almonds into small pieces. Put mixture in a pudding pan set inside of a pan of water and bake in oven one hour. Cover while cooking. Serve with cream.

Stonewall Jackson Pudding

2 cupsful of milk,
2 egg yolks,
1/2 cup of sugar,
2 tablespoonsful of Knox Gelatine softened in 1/4 cupful of cold milk,
1 teaspoonful of vanilla,
1/8 cupful of sherry wine,
2 egg whites,
1/2 pint of whipped cream.

Heat the milk to the boiling point in double boiler. Beat the yolks very light and beat into them the sugar. Add this to the hot milk and cook until the custard begins to get thick. Take from the fire. Add gelatine, which has been softened in one-fourth cupful of cold milk. Add vanilla and sherry wine and let cool. Beat the whites of eggs stiff, and fold into them the whipped cream. When custard begins to set, fold into it the cream and whites of eggs and put into a mold. Mold with alternate layers of broken macaroons and crystallized cherries.

Syllabub

1 pint of cream, rich and sweet,
1/2 cup of sugar,
1 cup of sherry wine,
1 teaspoonful of vanilla.

Sweeten the cream and when the sugar has dissolved, stir in the wine carefully. Add the vanilla and beat to a stiff froth. Serve in glasses.

U.D.C. Pudding

1 cup of finely chopped crystallized pineapple,
1 cup of finely chopped crystallized cherries,
1 cup of finely chopped nuts,
6 eggs.

Add a tablespoonful of sugar to each egg, beat well, leaving out the whites. To the yolks and sugar add one cup of sherry wine and cook to a thick custard in double boiler. To the custard while hot add one tablespoonful of gelatine dissolved in one-half cup of water, then whip in lightly the beaten whites. Roll out macaroons or Social Teas into dust. Into a bowl begin to lay cracker dust, pineapple, nuts and cherries. When you have used half the ingredients, pour over it the other half of the fruits and custard, sprinkling the top with cracker dust. Put into refrigerator to congeal. Serve with whipped cream (no sugar or flavoring in cream).

Rhubarb Pie

1 pint of rhubarb,
1 tablespoonful of flour,
1 cupful of sugar,
1/4 teaspoonful of soda.

Remove the skin, and cut into small pieces enough rhubarb to fill a pint bowl. Add the soda, and pour over it boiling water to cover. Let stand fifteen minutes and pour off the water. Line a deep plate with a rich crust. Put in the rhubarb, sugar and flour, cover with crust. Bake twenty minutes or half an hour.

Jeff Davis Custard

4 eggs, beaten separately,
1 cup of cream,
2 tablespoonsful of butter,
1 cups of sugar.

Flavor to taste. Pour the mixture on thin, rich crusts.

Cream Puffs

Stir one-half pound of butter into a pint of warm water, set it on the fire in a sauce pan and bring it to a boil, stirring often. When it boils put in three-fourths of a pound of flour and let boil one minute, stirring constantly. Take from the fire and turn into a deep dish to cool. Beat eight eggs light, and whip into this cool paste, first the yolks, then the whites. Drop in great spoonsful on buttered paper so as not to touch or run into each other, and bake ten minutes. Split them and fill with the following cream:

1 quart of milk,
4 tablespoonsful of cornstarch,
2 eggs,
2 cups sugar.

Stir while boiling and when thick, add a teaspoonful of butter. When cold, flavor.

Brown Betty

Pare and slice apples thin. Put alternate layers of apples and bread crumbs sprinkled with cinnamon, bits of butter, and brown sugar in buttered baking dish. Then add one cup of water and bake until apples are thoroughly done and brown on top.

Southern Apple Pie

6 apples,
Grated rind and juice of one lemon,
1/2 cup of sugar,
1 teaspoon cinnamon,
2 macaroons rolled,
1/4 teaspoon salt,
2 tablespoons butter,
2 eggs slightly beaten.

Pare and slice apples, add one-quarter cup of water. Cook until soft, and rub through a sieve. Add other ingredients in order given. Line a deep plate or patty tins with rich paste, fill, and bake about forty minutes. Cake crumbs may be substituted for macaroons.

Caramel Custard

Line a pie plate with nice pastry. For one custard allow one egg well beaten, one cup of brown sugar, four teaspoonsful of milk, one tablespoonful of flour or starch and a piece of butter the size of an egg. Pour this in the crust and bake. After baking make a meringue and bake a delicate brown.

Palmetto Marmalade

2 quarts of fresh pears ground fine,
2 cans of grated pineapple,
6 oranges cut into small pieces,

As many cups of sugar as there are cupsful of fruit. Put all together on to cook and cook until thick and a pretty red color.

Aunt Jemina's Lemon Pie

6 eggs,
1 1/2 cups of sugar,
2 tablespoonsful of butter,
3 lemons,
2 tablespoonsful of flour,
1/2 teaspoonful of baking powder,
1 cup of milk.

To well beaten yolks add sugar, flour, milk, butter, baking powder, juice and grated rind of three lemons. Cook in double boiler until thick and then bake on a nice crust. After baking, make a meringue of the whites and bake to a delicate brown.

Nut Bread

2 1/2 cupsful of flour,
3 teaspoonsful of baking powder,
1/4 teaspoonful of salt,
1/2 cupful of sugar,
1 egg,
1 cupful of milk,
3/4 cupful of English walnuts chopped fine.

Beat egg and sugar together, then add milk and salt. Sift the baking-powder into the dry flour, and put all the ingredients together. Add the nuts last, covering with a little flour, to prevent falling, and bake in a moderate oven one hour.

Chocolate Pudding

Put two squares of unsweetened chocolate in double boiler, add two cupsful of cold milk, and bring to the scalding point. Mix thoroughly one-fourth of a cupful of sugar, three tablespoonsful of cornstarch, one-fourth of a teaspoonful of salt and pour on one-fourth of a cupful of milk gradually, while stirring constantly. Add to milk which was scalded with chocolate, and cook fifteen minutes, stirring constantly until mixture thickens and afterward occasionally. Add one-half of a teaspoonful of vanilla and turn into a serving dish. Chill and serve.

Maryland Bread Pudding

1 pint of stale bread,
1 quart of milk,
1 cupful of sugar,
1 egg,
1/2 cupful of raisins,
1 teaspoonful of cinnamon,
1/2 teaspoonful of salt.

Pour hot water on the stale bread and let soak until soft. Then add other ingredients and bake for three hours in a moderate oven. If eaten cold, serve with hot sauce. If eaten hot, serve with cold sauce.

Sunset Raisin Pie

1 cup of seeded raisins chopped fine,
1 lemon with grated rind.

Add lemon juice and grated rind to the raisins. Then add one cup of sugar and two tablespoonsful of water. Bake between upper and lower crusts.

Soft Ginger Bread

1/2 cup of sugar,
1 cup of molasses,
1/2 cup of butter or lard,
1 teaspoonful each of ginger, cinnamon and cloves,
2 teaspoonsful of soda in a cup of boiling water,
2 1/2 cups of flour,
2 well beaten eggs added last.

Mix in the order given and bake in slow oven.

Sauce for Ginger Bread

1 cup of sugar,
1 tablespoonful of butter.

Creamed together. Add one-half cup of cream or milk and five tablespoonsful of wine. Stir constantly while cooking until dissolved and creamy. Flavor to taste with vanilla or nutmeg.

Cranberry Surprise

Crumble three lady fingers into a baking dish, cover with a thin layer of cranberry preserves or jelly. Dot with small lumps of butter and add a sprinkle of cinnamon. Beat three eggs separately very light and add two cups of milk. Pour over the fruit and cake. Bake as a custard and serve with whipped cream.

Louisiana Molasses Custard

Mix well the yolks of two eggs, one cup of molasses, one scant cup of sugar, one cup of buttermilk with pinch of soda and two tablespoonsful of flour. Flavor with cinnamon and vanilla. Cook in double boiler until thick, then bake on a rich pie crust. Use the whites for meringue.

Jellied Apples

Put on four cups of sugar and four cups of water with six cloves and bring to boiling point.

Peel and core apples and drop them into boiling syrup. Cover kettle and let apples steam slowly until they are clear and tender. Pour last of syrup over fruit and serve.

Mammy's Sweet Potato Pudding

Grate three medium sized potatoes. Beat together one cup of sugar, three eggs, one tablespoonful of butter, one pint of milk, and add to the grated potato.

Pour in a buttered pan, drop bits of butter on top and bake one hour in a moderate oven. Flavor with one teaspoonful of vanilla.

Raisin Rolls

1 1/2 cupsful of flour,
1/2 cupful of lard (scant)
1/2 teaspoonful of salt,
1 cupful of raisins,
1 cracker,
1 lemon,
2/3 cupful of sugar,
1 egg,
A little salt.

Beat the egg, add sugar, salt, lemon juice and grated rind. Roll cracker fine, chop raisins and mix all together. Roll the crust thin, cut into rounds. Put a spoonful of filling between two rounds and pinch the edges together. Prick top crust with fork. Bake in iron pan for twenty minutes.

New Orleans Dark Nut Bread

1/4 cup of sugar,
3/4 cup hot water,
1/2 cup molasses,
1/4 cup milk,
2 cups entire wheat flour,
1 cup bread flour,
5 teaspoons baking powder,
1 1/2 teaspoons salt,
1/2 teaspoon soda,
3/4 cup nut meats, finely chopped.

Mix in order given, sifting dry materials together before adding. Turn into a greased bread pan, let stand fifteen minutes, and bake in a moderate oven one hour.

Baked Apple Dumplings

Take rich pie crust, roll thin as for pie and cut into rounds as large as a tea plate. Pare and slice fine one small apple for each dumpling. Lay the apple on the crust, sprinkle on a tiny bit of sugar and nutmeg, turn edges of crust over the apple and press together. Bake in a hot oven for twenty minutes. Serve hot with cold sauce.

Virginia Dare Pudding

Sift one quart of flour and into the flour put one pound of raisins, one pound of currants, one-half teaspoonful of salt, one pound of sugar, one grated nutmeg, and one teaspoonful of ground spice. Beat four eggs and add after mixing the fruit well in the flour, and mix with enough water to make a stiff batter as for fruit cake. Boil or bake and serve with sauce. Cook for about two hours.

Sweet Potato Custard

3 cooked sweet potatoes,
1/4 nutmeg grated,
2 eggs,
1/4 cup brown sugar,
1/3 teaspoon salt,
1 quart milk.

Force potatoes through a ricer. Beat the eggs and mix with potatoes. Add other ingredients, pour into buttered baking dish or cups, and bake in a slow oven until firm.

Banana Custard

Mix well the yolks of 2 eggs,
1/2 cup of sweet milk,
1/2 cup of sugar,
1 teaspoonful of butter,
2 tablespoonsful of flour.

Cook in double boiler until thick. When cool, add one teaspoonful of vanilla. Bake on a nice crust. When cool, cover pie with thin slices of banana, then the meringue, and bake a delicate brown.

Strawberry Shortcake

Make regular pie crust and roll it into two sheets, each about one-half inch thick. Bake in well-greased pan, laying one sheet on top of the other. When done and while warm separate them. When cold put between the crusts a thick layer of strawberries well sprinkled with powdered sugar. Arrange largest berries on top. Cut in wedge-shaped pieces and serve with sweetened whipped cream.

Tapioca Custard

One quart of milk and one cup of soaked and drained tapioca should be placed in a double boiler and cooked until the tapioca is transparent. Then add one cup of sugar and the yolks of three well beaten eggs. Let it cook for a few minutes, flavor as desired and pour into a bowl. Cover the top with the whites of the eggs beaten stiff and sweetened.

Bavarian Cream

One quart of sweet cream whipped with two cups of sugar as stiff as for syllabub, two-thirds of a box of gelatine dissolved over the fire in two cups of milk, stirring constantly. Let cool. Flavor cream to taste, then beat in the milk and gelatine. If desired, fruits, nuts, and maraschino cherries may be added.

Cranberry Snow

Whip stiff the white of one egg and add alternately and gradually three tablespoonsful of sugar and a cup of cranberry sauce. Continue to whip until it has reached at least a pint and a half in quantity, for it swells surprisingly. Finely chopped nuts may be added if desired.

Chocolate Pie

1/4 cake of chocolate,
2 cups of sugar,
1/2 cup of butter,
4 eggs,
1 tablespoon of flour.

Beat yolks together with butter, sugar, milk and flour. Cook in double boiler until thick, then bake on a nice crust. Use whites for meringue.

Pumpkin Pie

2 cupsful of stewed and sifted pumpkin,
2 crackers rolled fine,
1 cupful of sugar,
Pinch of salt,
1/2 teaspoonful of cinnamon,
1 pint of milk,

Pour the mixture into a deep pie-plate lined with crust, and bake in a slow oven one hour.

SALADS AND DRESSINGS

☆　☆　☆　☆

Mayonnaise Dressing (Without Oil)

Mix together two tablespoonsful of flour, one teaspoonful of mustard, one teaspoonful of salt, one tablespoonful of sugar. Add this to two eggs well beaten, and lastly one cup of vinegar. Put on to cook in a double boiler and cook until thick, stirring frequently.

Maryland Chicken Salad

Boil one large chicken until tender, and when cold cut in dice. To diced chicken add four hard boiled eggs mashed fine, one and a half bunches of celery chopped fine, and salt and pepper to taste. Mix well with oil dressing and the juice of one lemon.

Potato Salad

5 medium sized, cold, boiled Irish potatoes, diced
3 hard boiled eggs,
A few pieces of parsley chopped fine,
1 cup of diced celery.

Season with salt, black and red pepper and mix well with oil dressing.

Wesson Oil Dressing

Yolks of 3 eggs,
1/2 teaspoon of salt,
1/4 teaspoon of mustard,
1/4 teaspoon of red pepper,
Juice of 1 lemon,
Pint of Wesson oil.

Beat yolks until thick; then add salt, pepper, mustard and part of lemon juice. Lastly add the oil one drop at a time at first, then slowly until dressing is thick, and then the remainder of the lemon juice.

Tomato Jelly

Cover one-half box of gelatine with one and one-half cups of cold water. Stew one quart can of tomatoes until tender and strain. Season with salt, pepper and sugar to taste and bring to boiling point. Pour hot tomato juice into the melted gelatine and add to this one hard boiled egg sliced thin. One small bottle of stuffed olives sliced thin and one-half cup of nuts. Pour into small molds wet with cold water and serve on lettuce with oil dressing.

French Dressing

2/3 cup oil,
1/2 teaspoon pepper,
1/3 cup vinegar,
1/4 teaspoon mustard,
1 1/4 teaspoons salt,
1 teaspoon powdered sugar.

Put the ingredients in a pint preserve jar. Fasten the cover, chill and shake well before using. Keep in the ice-box and use as needed. For use with fruit salad, omit mustard. Curry, Brand's A-1 sauce, Worchestershire sauce, tomato ketchup, or similar condiments may be added in small amounts to vary the flavor.

Waldorf Salad

2 cups of apples peeled and diced,
2 cups of celery,
1 cup of nuts.

Mix well together with oil dressing.

Shrimp Salad

3 cups cooked shrimp, minced,
1/4 cup chopped olives,
1 cup mayonnaise,
1 cup chopped celery,
2 tablespoons chopped pimento,
1/2 cup French dressing.

Marinate shrimp in French dressing. Drain, add celery, olives and pimento. Mix with mayonnaise and fill tomato cases, putting a teaspoon mayonnaise on each. Serve on leaf of head lettuce.

Pineapple and Cottage Cheese Salad

For each person allow two lettuce leaves, one slice of pineapple and three dates stuffed with cream cheese. Cut the pineapple into cubes and place on the lettuce. Cut the dates in halves lengthwise, remove stones, stuff with cream cheese and arrange on the pineapple. Sprinkle cheese with paprika and dress all with French dressing.

Water Lily Salad

6 hard boiled eggs,
Mayonnaise dressing,
Lettuce.

Cut the white of each egg into six long petals. Arrange the pieces in circular form on the lettuce. Form the center of each lily by putting in the yolks, well mixed with mayonnaise.

Marshmallow Salad

Cut into small pieces marshmallows, white grapes, sliced pineapple, almonds or pecans and a little banana, sliced thin. Serve on lettuce with oil dressing and maraschino cherries to garnish it.

Frozen Fruit Salad

2 cans of white cherries,
1 can of sliced pineapple,
1 can of pears,
6 oranges,
3 pints of cream,
2 pints of dressing.

Whip the cream, sweeten and flavor to taste. Mix the cream and the dressing. Put in the fruit, but do not use the juice of the fruit. Pack the mixture in coffee or baking powder cans and let them remain in ice four or five hours. A small tub can be used to set the cans in and pack ice and salt around them.

SOUPS

Old Virginia Brunswick Stew

Boil one chicken and one rabbit or squirrel in two or three quarts of water. When about half done add one quart of lima beans, one quart of tomatoes, one quart of corn and butter the size of two eggs. Season to taste with salt and pepper and cook until thick enough to eat with a fork.

Aunt Caroline's Porridge

Pick over and wash two-thirds of a cupful of white beans. Put on the back of the stove in cold water. Let these boil slowly, while the dinner is cooking. When the boiled dinner has been taken up, put these beans into the liquor in which the dinner was cooked. Boil one hour. Wet three tablespoonsful of flour with water, and stir in while boiling, to thicken. Serve hot, adding a little milk if desired.

Cream of Celery Soup

3 stalks of celery, chopped fine,
1 slice of onion,
3 cupfuls of milk.

Boil for twenty minutes, then add three tablespoonsful of melted butter. Thicken with three tablespoonsful of flour dissolved in a little milk. Add salt and pepper to taste, then one cupful of cream and serve hot.

Tomato Bisque

Put a quart of tomatoes in a kettle and boil for about twenty minutes, or until juice is thick. Season with salt, pepper and sugar to taste, then add one-half teaspoonful of soda. Strain and add to hot strained juice one pint of scalded milk. Boil a few minutes and serve with oyster crackers or squares of toast.

Tomato Soup Creole Style

1 quart of tomatoes,
1 tablespoonful of butter,
1 tablespoonful of flour,
1 onion,
Sprig of parsley,
Salt and pepper to taste.

Put tomatoes, onion, parsley, salt and pepper on to cook. When cooling add flour and butter which have been creamed together. Cook until thick.

Dixie Land Soup

4 potatoes,
3 pints of milk,
Piece of butter size of an egg,
Small piece of onion.

Take four large potatoes, boil until done and mash smooth, adding butter and salt to taste. Heat the milk in a double boiler, cook the onion in it a few minutes and then remove. Pour the milk slowly on the potato, strain, heat and serve immediately. Thicken with one tablespoonful of flour.

Cream of Tomato

Put a quart of tomatoes in a kettle, add one cupful of water and boil for about ten minutes; season with salt, pepper, and sugar to taste, then add one-half teaspoonful of soda. When the tomatoes have boiled, strain them and add to the strained juice one pint of scalded milk. Lastly add one cupful of cream in which a little flour has been blended.

Baltimore Oyster Stew

25 oysters,
1 teaspoonful of flour,
1 quart of milk,
Butter,
Salt.

Take twenty-five oysters, with their liquor and put these into an agate dish on the stove with salt to taste, in a pint of cold water. Boil five minutes. Stir into this one heaping teaspoonful of flour, which has been wet with two tablespoonsful of cold water. Add one quart of milk. Let it come to a boil, but be sure not to have it boil. Remove from the fire, and add a piece of butter the size of an egg. This is sufficient for eight people.

Cream of Pea Soup

1 can peas,
1 1/4 teaspoons salt,
1 slice onion,
1/8 teaspoon pepper,
Bit of bay leaf,
2 cups boiling water,
Sprig of parsley,
2 cups hot milk,
1 teaspoon sugar,
1 tablespoon butter,
2 tablespoons flour.

Rinse the peas with cold water, and reserve one-fourth cup. Simmer the remainder with seasonings and hot water, for twenty minutes, and press through a sieve. Thicken the milk with butter and flour blended together, and add to peas. Add the whole peas just before serving.

Cream of Chicken Soup

3 cups of chicken stock,
Salt,
1 slice onion,
1/8 teaspoon pepper,
1/4 cup celery tops,
2 tablespoons chicken fat or butter,
1 cup hot milk,
3 tablespoons flour.

Cook stock, onion, and celery for fifteen minutes, and strain. Add hot milk and seasonings, and thicken with chicken fat and flour blended together. The amount of salt will depend upon the quantity in the stock. Celery salt may be used in place of celery tops.

Oatmeal Soup

3/4 cup cooked oatmeal,
2 cups hot milk,
1/2 onion sliced,
1 teaspoon salt,
2 cloves,

1/8 teaspoon celery salt,
1/2 bay leaf,
1/8 teaspoon pepper,
2 cups boiling water,
1/2 tablespoon butter.

Cook oatmeal, onion, cloves, and bay leaf in boiling water for twenty minutes, and press through a sieve. Add milk, seasonings, and butter, and serve with croutons.

VEGETABLES

General Pickett Corn Pudding

1 pint of fresh corn, or 1 can of corn,
2 eggs,
1 cup of sweet milk,
1 cup of sugar,
Butter the size of an egg,
Little salt,
1 tablespoonful of flour,
1/4 teaspoonful of baking powder.

Mix well together, leaving out whites for meringue. Pour into baking dish and cook in hot oven. When cool, beat whites of eggs stiff, sweeten and flavor, spread on top of pudding and bake a delicate brown.

Dixie Potatoes

4 or 5 baked potatoes,
1 pint of milk,
1/2 teaspoonful of salt,
Butter, the size of a walnut.

Pare the potatoes and cut into small pieces. Put them on the stove, in an agate dish, salt and cover with milk. Let them cook fifteen or twenty minutes, then thicken with one tablespoonful of flour, stirred with half a cupful of water; put in the butter and serve hot.

Southern Creamed Sweet Potatoes

To two cups of mashed sweet potatoes add one teaspoonful of cinnamon, one cup of sweet milk, one-half cup of sugar, one-half cup of seeded raisins and butter size of an egg. Cook in buttered baking dish and when done, cool, spread the top with marshmallows and brown in oven.

Stuffed Potatoes With Cheese

Select large Irish potatoes and bake. When done cut in half, take meat of potato from shell, mix with little salt, pepper and grated cheese. Put back in shell, put butter on top and bake until light brown.

Scalloped Irish Potatoes

Cut raw potatoes into small cubes and put into baking dish. Add salt, pepper and pieces of butter. Cover with sweet milk and cook in the oven.

Stuffed Tomatoes

Peel large ripe tomatoes and cut in quarters. Place in the center of each tomato one tablespoonful of ground stuffed olives, one teaspoonful of ground, hard boiled egg, and one teaspoonful of English walnuts or pecans. Serve on lettuce with oil dressing and grated cheese sprinkled on top of dressing.

Scalloped Tomatoes in Shells

Peel as many, fresh tomatoes as persons to serve. Make small round opening at the top by hollowing with a teaspoon. Season highly with mayonnaise, catsup, mustard and enough crab flake to fill the tomatoes, Set on ice and serve very cold for luncheon.

Aunt Katy's Macaroni

1/2 small sized package of macaroni,
1/3 pound cheese,
1 cup of milk,
Butter the size of a walnut,
1/2 cup of bread crumbs.

Put macaroni on to boil in water with a little salt. When tender drain off water. Put in a baking dish first a layer of macaroni, then cheese, crumbs and butter. Pour milk over it and bake.

Irish Potato Puffs

2 cups of cold mashed potatoes,
2 tablespoonsful of melted butter.

Beat together until smooth, and add two well beaten eggs and one cup of sweet milk. Pour into a baking dish, bake quickly and serve immediately.

Stewed Celery

Wash four heads and take off the green leaves. Cut into pieces three or four inches long, put into a stew-pan with one-half pint of meat broth, stew till tender. Add a little cream and seasoning; also a little flour and butter, and simmer together.

Baked Tomatoes

Take out from the top the inside of large tomatoes, with this mix bread crumbs, butter, pepper, salt, a little sugar and some chopped onions. Fill the tomatoes with this, set them in a deep dish or plate and bake slowly for one half-hour.

Mammy's Candies Sweet Potatoes

Boil six small sized sweet potatoes, peel them and lay on a shallow plate or pan. Put a teaspoon butter on each potato, sprinkle on them one half-cup of brown sugar, two tablespoons water in pan, cook slowly and baste as you would meat. Cinnamon, cloves, nutmeg, and lemon peel improve the flavor.

Boiled Turnips

Cut up five or six flat white turnips and chop fine in a chopping-bowl. Put into boiling water and cook till tender. Drain off the water, add sufficient seasoning and one half-cup good vinegar. Let them simmer on the stove about ten minutes. These are excellent.

Stewed Green Corn

Cut the corn off the cob, boil in little water fifteen or twenty minutes. When done, add a cup of milk or cream, a little butter, and season to taste.

Creole Potato Balls

Mash some mealy potatoes smooth, season, and add butter and cream till quite moist. Make up into balls, dip in beaten eggs, roll in bread crumbs, and fry in butter to a nice brown.

Potato Chips

Pare the potatoes, shave them very thin and soak for one half-hour in ice-cold salted water. Drain in a colander, and spread upon a dry towel. Fry a few at a time in very hot fat, one minute being sufficient to cook and brown them properly, sprinkle lightly with salt, and when needed at table, heat quickly in the oven.

Stuffed Potatoes With Cheese and Bacon

4 large potatoes,
3/4 teaspoon salt,
4 tablespoons grated cheese,
1/4 teaspoon paprika,
1/4 cup hot milk,
4 slices bacon.

Wash potatoes and bake in a hot oven forty-five minutes. Cut in halves lengthwise, remove potato, and force through potato ricer. Add cheese, seasonings, and hot milk. Beat vigorously, and refill potato skins. Place half a slice of bacon on top of each, and put on the upper grate of a hot oven until bacon is crisp.

Jenny Lind Potatoes

4 large, cold, boiled potatoes, peeled and sliced,
2 tablespoons butter,
1 pint hot milk,
2 tablespoons flour.

Melt butter and add hot milk and flour, when thick add salt, pepper and parsley. Put a layer of mixture in bottom of baking dish, then a layer of potato, and so on; milk coming last. Cover with cracker crumbs and bake fifteen minutes.

Carolina Sweet Potato Pone

One quart sweet potatoes, peeled and grated; pour over the grated potato one pint boiling water, stir it well. Add one tea-cup brown sugar, two tea-cups molasses, two tablespoons butter. One heaping tablespoon powdered ginger, one tea-cup milk. Pour into a baking dish and bake slowly for about two hours.

Scalloped Potatoes

Butter a baking-dish, pare and slice potatoes in small pieces. Put into the dish with salt, pepper and a little butter. Fill the dish with milk, sprinkle over the top cracker, or bread crumbs, and cheese if you like it. Bake in the oven for an hour and a half or two hours.

French Fried Sweet Potatoes

Cut cold boiled sweet potatoes into eighths lengthwise, fry in deep fat until brown, drain on soft paper, and sprinkle with salt.

Fried Egg Plant

Cut a small egg plant in one-third-inch slices; pare; cut each slice in quarters. Soak in cold salted water for half an hour; drain. Season with pepper and salt, dip in crumbs, then in egg, and then in crumbs again; and fry in deep fat about three minutes. Or dip in flour and saute in butter.

CONFEDERATE RECEIPT BOOK

A Compilation of Over
One Hundred Receipts
Adapted to the Times

THE CONFEDERATE
REPRINT COMPANY
☆ ☆ ☆ ☆
WWW.CONFEDERATEREPRINT.COM

ADVERTISEMENT

The accompanying receipts have been compiled and published with a view to present to the public in a form capable of preservation and easy reference many valuable receipts which have appeared in the Southern newspapers since the commencement of the war. With these have been incorporated receipts and hints derived from other sources, all designed to supply useful and economical directions and suggestions in cookery, housewifery, &c., and for the camp. Should the present publication meet with favor, another edition with additional receipts will be published, contributions to which will be thankfully received by

The Publishers

CULINARY RECEIPTS

☆　☆　☆　☆

Biscuit

Take one quart of flour, three teaspoonfuls of cream of tartar, mixed well through the flour, two tablespoonfuls of shortening, one teaspoonful of soda, dissolved in warm water, of sufficient quantity to mould the quart of flour. For large families the amount can be doubled.

Another Receipt

Take two quarts of flour, two ounces of butter, half pint of boiling water, one teaspoonful of salt, one pint of cold milk, and half cup yeast. Mix well and set to rise, then mix a teaspoonful of saleratus in a little water and mix into dough, roll on a board an inch thick, cut into small biscuits, and bake twenty minutes.

Soda Biscuit

One quart of sour milk, one teaspoonful of soda, one of salt, a piece of butter the size of an egg, and flour enough to make them roll out.

Pumpkin Bread

Boil a good pumpkin in water till it is quite thick, pass it through a sieve, and mix flour so as to make a good dough. This makes an excellent bread.

Nice Buns

Take three quarters of a pound of sifted flour, two large spoonfuls of brown sugar, two spoonfuls of good yeast, add a little salt, stir well together, and when risen work in two spoonfuls of butter, make into buns, set it to rise again, and bake on tins.

Indian Bread

One quart of butter milk, one quart of corn meal, one quart of coarse flour, one cup of molasses, add a little soda and salt.

To Raise Bread Without Yeast

Mix in your flour subcarbonate of soda, two parts, tartaric acid one part, both finely powdered. Mix up your bread with warm water, adding but little at a time, and bake soon.

Yeast

Boil one pound of good flour, a quarter of a pound of brown sugar and a little salt in two gallons of water for one hour. When milk warm bottle it close, it will be fit to use in twenty four hours. One part of this will make eighteen pounds of bread.

A Cheap and Quick Pudding

Beat up four eggs, add a pint of milk and little salt, and stir in four large spoonfuls of flour, a little nutmeg and sugar to your taste. Beat it well, and pour it into buttered teacups, filling them rather more than half full. They will bake in a stove or Dutch oven in fifteen minutes.

Republican Pudding

Take one cup of soft boiled rice, a pint of milk, a cup of sugar, three eggs, and a piece of butter the size of an egg. Serve with sauce.

A Minute Pudding

Stir flour into boiling milk to the consistence of a thin hasty pudding, and in fifteen or twenty minutes it will be fit for the table. Serve with sauce to suit the taste.

Peas Pudding

Take about three quarters of a pint of split peas, and put them into a pint basin, tie a cloth over them (to give room to swell,) put them into *boiling water*, and let them boil two hours, then take them up, untie them, add an egg beaten up, a little butter, with salt and pepper, then beat up, tie up again, and place them in the water to boil for about twenty minutes more, you will then have a well flavored and nice shaped pudding.

Plain Potato Pudding

Having pared a pound of fine large potatoes, put them into a pot, cover them well with cold water, and boil them gently till tender all through. When done lay each potato (one at a time) in a clean warm napkin, and press and wring it till all the moisture is squeezed out, and the potato becomes a round dry lump. Mince as fine as possible a quarter of a pound of fresh beef suet, (divested of skin and strings;) crumble the potato and mix it well with the suet; adding a small salt spoon of salt. Add sufficient milk to make a thick batter, and beat it well. Dip a strong square cloth in hot water, shake it out, and dredge it well with flour. Tie the pudding in, leaving room for it to swell, and put it into a large pot of hot water, and boil it steady for an hour. This is a good and economical pudding.

Potato Crust

Boil six good-sized mealy potatoes, and mash them fine, add salt, a spoonful of butter, and two of water, while they are hot, then work in flour enough for making a paste to roll out, or put in two or three spoonfuls of cream, and no butter or water. This is a good crust for hot pies or dumplings.

Paste For Pies

Excellent paste for fruit or meat pies may be made with two-thirds of wheat flour, one-third of the flour of boiled potatoes, and some butter or dripping, the whole being brought to a proper consistence with warm water, and a small quantity of yeast added when lightness is desired. This will also make palatable cakes for breakfast, and may be made with or without spices, fruit, &c.

Apple Pie Without Apples

To one small bowl of crackers, that have been soaked until no hard parts remain, add one teaspoonful of tartaric acid, sweeten to your taste, add some butter, and a very little nutmeg.

Artificial Oysters

Take young green corn, grate it in a dish; to one pint of this add one egg, well beaten, a small teacup of flour, two or three tablespoonfuls of butter, some salt and pepper, mix them all together. A tablespoonful of the batter will make the size of an oyster. Fry them light brown, and when done butter them. Cream if it can be procured is better.

Cottage Cheese

This is a good way of using up a pan of milk that is found to be turning sour. Having covered it, set it in a warm place till it becomes a curd, then pour off the liquid, and tie up the curd in a clean linen bag with a pointed end, and set a bowl under it to catch the droppings, but do not squeeze it. After it has drained ten or twelve hours transfer the curd to a deep dish, enrich it with some cream, and press and chop it with a large spoon till it is a soft mass, adding as you proceed an ounce or more of nice fresh butter.

Slapjacks

Take flour, little sugar and water, mix with or without a little yeast, the latter better if at hand, mix into paste, and fry the same as fritters in clean fat.

Indian Sagamite

Three parts of Indian meal and one of brown sugar, mixed and browned over the fire, will make the food known as "Sagamite." Used in small quantities, it not only appeases hunger but allays thirst, and is therefore useful to soldiers on a scout.

BEER, VINEGAR, &c.

☆　☆　☆　☆

Table Beer

To eight quarts of boiling water put a pound of treacle, a quarter of an ounce of ginger and two bay leaves, let this boil for a quarter of an hour, then cool, and work it with yeast as other beer.

Another Receipt

Eight quarts water, one quart molasses, one pint yeast, one tablespoonful cream of tartar, mixed and bottled in twenty-four hours; or, to two pounds of coarse brown sugar add two gallons of water, and nearly two ounces hops. Let the whole boil three quarters of an hour, and then work as usual It should stand a week or ten days before being drawn, and will improve daily afterward for a moderate time.

Spruce Beer

Take three gallons of water, blood warmth, three half pints of molasses, a tablespoonful of essence of spruce, and the like quantity of ginger, mix well together with a gill of yeast, let it stand over night, and bottle it in the morning. It will be in a good condition to drink in twenty-four hours.

Ginger Beer

One pint of molasses and two spoonfuls of ginger put into a pail, to be half filled with boiling water; when well stirred together, fill the pail with cold water, leaving room for one pint of yeast, which must not be put in until lukewarm. Place it on a warm hearth for the night, and bottle in the morning.

Blackberry Wine

Measure your berries and bruise them; to every gallon add one quart of boiling water, let the mixture stand twenty-four hours, stirring occasionally, then strain off the liquor into a cask; to every gallon add two pounds of sugar, cork tight, and let it stand till following October, and you will have wine ready for use without any further straining or boiling, that will make lips smack as they never smacked under similar influence before.

Apple Water

Take one tart apple of ordinary size, well baked, let it be well mashed, pour on it one pint of boiling water, beat them well together, let it stand to cool, and strain it off for use. It may be sweetened with sugar if desired.

Cider Jelly

Boil cider to the consistence of syrup, and let it cool, and you have nice jelly.

To Make Vinegar

Take one pint of molasses, put it in a jug with one gallon of warm water, not boiling, let it stand for two months, and you will have good vinegar.

Another Receipt For a Larger Quantity

To eight gallons of clear rain water add three quarts of molasses, put into a good cask shake well a few times, then add two or three spoonfuls of good yeast. If in the summer place the cask in the sun; if in winter near the chimney, where it may be warm. In ten or fifteen days add to the liquid a sheet of brown paper, torn in strips, dipped into molasses, and good vinegar will be produced.

Tomato Catsup

Nice catsup may be made with four quarts of tomatoes, one pint of vinegar, three table spoonfuls salt, two of mustard, two of black pepper, three red peppers broken and half ounce allspice or mace.

SOAP AND CANDLES

Soap

Pour twelve quarts of boiling water upon five pounds of unslacked lime. Then dissolve five pounds of washing soda in twelve quarts of boiling water, mix the above together, and let the mixture remain from twelve to twenty-four hours, for the purpose of chemical action. Now pour off all the clear liquid, being careful not to disturb the sediment. Add to the above three and a half pounds of clarified grease, and from three to four ounces of rosin. Boil this compound together for one hour, and pour off to cool. Cut it up in bars for use, and you are in the possession of a superior chemical soap, costing about three and a half cents per pound in ordinary times.

Soft Soap

Bore some holes in a lye barrel, put some straw in the bottom, lay some unslacked lime on it, and fill your barrel with good hard wood ashes, wet it, and pound it down as you put it in. When full, make a basin in the ashes and pour in water, keep filling it as it sinks in the ashes. In the course of a few hours the lye will begin to run. When you have a sufficient quantity to begin with, put your grease in a large iron pot, pour in the lye, let it boil, &c. Three pounds of clean grease are allowed for two gallons of soap.

Honey Soap

Cut into thin shavings two pounds of common yellow or white soap, put it on the fire with just water enough to keep it from burning; when quite melted, add a quarter of a pound of honey, stirring it till it boils, then take it off and add a few drops of any agreeable perfume. Pour it into a deep dish to cool, and then cut it into squares. It improves by keeping. It will soften and whiten the skin.

Tallow Candles

After melting the tallow, add say one pound of quicklime to every twenty of tallow, strain the tallow, and mould the candles. If this recipe is followed, you will have a candle equal to the adamantine, free from all impurities, and giving a brilliant light.

Confederate Candle

Melt together a pound of beeswax and a quarter of a pound of rosin or of turpentine, fresh from the tree. Prepare a wick 30 or 40 yards long, made up of three threads of loosely spun cotton, saturate this well with the mixture, and draw it through your fingers, to press all closely together, and to keep the size even. Repeat the process until the candle attains the size of a large straw or quill, then wrap around a bottle, or into a ball with a flat bottom. Six inches of this candle elevated above the rest will burn for fifteen or twenty minutes, and give a very pretty light, and forty yards have sufficed a small family a summer for all the usual purposes of the bed-chamber.

REMEDIES, &c.

☆ ☆ ☆ ☆

For Dysentery

Dissolve as much table salt in *pure* vinegar as will ferment and work clear. When the foam is discharged cork it up in a bottle, and put it away for use. A large spoonful of this in a gill of boiling water is efficacious in cases of dysentery and cholic.

Cure For Chills

The plant, commonly called hoarhound, is said to afford a certain cure. Boil it in water, and drink freely of the tea.

Gargle For Sore Throat, Diptheria or Scarlet Fever

Mix in a common size cup of fresh milk two teaspoonfuls of pulverized charcoal and ten drops of spirits of turpentine. Soften the charcoal with a few drops of milk before putting into the cup. Gargle frequently, according to the violence of the symptoms.

To Relieve Asthma

Take the leaves of the stramonium (or Jamestown weed,) dried in the shade, saturated with a pretty strong solution of salt petre, and smoke it so as to inhale the fumes. It may strangle at first if taken too freely, but it will loosen the phlegm in the lungs. The leaves should be gathered before frost.

Simple Cure For Croup

If a child is taken with croup apply cold water suddenly and freely to the neck and chest with a sponge or towel. The breathing will instantly be relieved, then wipe it dry, cover it up warm, and soon a quiet slumber will relieve the parent's anxiety.

For a Troublesome Cough

Take of treacle and the best white wine vinegar six tablespoonfuls each, add forty drops of laudanum, mix it well, and put into a bottle. A teaspoonful to be taken occasionally when the cough is troublesome. The mixture will be found efficacious without the laudanum in many cases.

For a Sick Headache

One teaspoonful of pulverized charcoal and one-third of a teaspoonful of soda mixed in very warm water.

Cure For a Toothache

Powdered alum will not only relieve the tooth-ache, but prevent the decay of the tooth. Salt may advantageously be mixed with the alum.

Cure For a Burn

Wheat flour and cold water, mixed to the consistency of soft paste, is an almost instantaneous cure for a burn. Renew before the first gets dry so as to stick.

Cure For Camp Itch

Take iodide of potassium, sixty grains, lard, two ounces, mix well, and after washing the body well with warm soap suds rub the ointment over the person three times a week. In seven or eight days the acarus or itch insect will be destroyed. In this recipe the horrible effects of the old sulphur ointment are obviated.

Cure For a Felon

The *Selma Reporter* says: A poultice of onions, applied morning, noon and night for three or four days, will cure a felon. No matter how bad the case, splitting the finger will be unnecessary, if this poultice be used. We have seen it tried several times, and know that the remedy is a sure, safe and speedy one.

To Cure Corns

The cause of corns, and likewise the pain they occasion, is simply friction, and to lessen the friction you have only to use your toe as you do in like circumstances a coach wheel – lubricate it with some oily substance. The best thing to use is a little sweet oil rubbed on the affected part (after the corn is carefully pared) with the tip of the finger, which should be done on getting up in the morning, and just before stepping into bed at night. In a few days the pain will diminish, and in a few days more it will cease, when the nightly application may be discontinued.

To Destroy Warts

Dissolve as much common washing soda as the water will take up, wash the warts with this for a minute or two, and let them dry without wiping. Keep the water in a bottle and repeat the washing often, and it will take away the largest of warts.

MISCELLANEOUS RECEIPTS

☆　☆　☆　☆

Preserving Meat Without Salt

We need salt as a relish to our food, but it is not essential in the preservation of our meats. The Indians used little or no salt, yet they preserved meat and even fish in abundance by drying. This can be accomplished by fire, by smoke or by sunshine, but the most rapid and reliable mode is by all these agents combined. To do this select a spot having the fullest command of sunshine. Erect there a wigwam five or six feet high, with an open top, in size proportioned to the quantity of meat to be cured, and protected from the winds, so that all the smoke must pass through the open top. The meat cut into pieces suitable for drying (the thinner the better) to be suspended on rods in the open comb, and a vigorous smoke made of decayed wood is to be kept up without cessation Exposed thus to the combined influence of sunshine, heat and smoke, meat cut into slices not over an inch thick can be thoroughly cured in twenty-four hours. For thicker pieces there must be, of course, a longer time, and the curing of oily meat, such as pork, is more difficult than that of beef, venison or mutton.

To cure meat *in the sun* hang it on the South side of your house, as near to the wall as possible without touching.

Savages *cure fish* by pounding it fine, and exposing it to the bright sun.

To Cure Bacon With Little Salt

Take five gallons water, seven pounds salt, one pound sugar, or one pint molasses, one teaspoonful saltpetre, mix, and after sprinkling the flesh side of the hams in the salt, pack in a tight barrel, hams first, then shoulders, lastly middlings. Pour over the brine, and if not enough to cover, make another draft of the above, and repeat till all is covered, leaving the meat in brine from four to seven weeks, according to size.

To Prevent Skippers in Ham

In order to avoid the skipper, and all worms and bugs that usually infest and destroy bacon, keep your smoke house *dark*, and the moth that deposits the eggs will never enter it. Smoke with green hickory, this is important, as the flavor of the bacon is often destroyed by smoking with improper wood.

Method of Curing Bad Butter

Melt the butter in hot water, skim it off as clean as possible, and work it over again in a churn, add salt and fine sugar, and press well.

To Clarify Molasses

To free molasses from its sharp taste, and to render it fit to be used, instead of sugar, take twelve pounds of molasses, twelve pounds of water, and three pounds of charcoal, coarsely pulverized, mix them in a kettle, and boil the whole over a slow wood fire. When the mixture has boiled half an hour, pour it into a flat vessel, in order that the charcoal may subside to the bottom, then pour off the liquid, and place it over the fire once more, that the superfluous water may evaporate, and the molasses be brought to their former consistence. Twelve pounds of molasses will produce twelve pounds of syrup.

Substitute For Cream in Tea or Coffee

Beat the white of an egg to a froth, put to it a very small lump of butter, and mix well, then turn the coffee to it gradually, so that it may not curdle. If perfectly done it will be an excellent substitute for cream. For tea omit the butter, using only the egg.

Substitute For Coffee

Take sound ripe acorns, wash them while in the shell, dry them, and parch until they open, take the shell off, roast with a little bacon fat, and you will have a splendid cup of coffee.

To Judge the Quality of Lamb

If fresh the vein in the neck of a forequarter is bluish; if green or yellow it is stale. In the hindquarter if the knuckle is limp, and the part under the kidney smells slightly disagreeable, avoid it. If the eyes are sunken do not buy the head.

To Test Flour

Knead a small quantity by way of experiment. If good, the flour immediately forms an adhesive elastic paste, which will readily assume any form that may be given to it without breaking.

To Prepare Salt

Set a lump of salt in a plate before the fire, and when dry pound it in a mortar, or rub two pieces of salt together. It will then be free from lumps, and in very fine powder.

Soft Water

If you are troubled to get soft water for washing fill a tub or barrel half full of wood ashes, and fill it up with water, so that you may have lye whenever you want it. A gallon of strong lye put into a large kettle of hard water will make it as soft as rain water.

Nutmegs

The largest, heaviest, and most unctuous nutmegs are the best. If you begin to grate nutmeg at the stalk end it will prove hollow throughout.

Rice Glue

Mix rice flour smoothly with cold water, and simmer it over a slow fire, when it will form a delicate and durable cement, not only answering all the purposes of common paste, but well adapted for joining paper and card board ornamental work.

To Cement Broken China or Glass

Beat lime to the finest powder, and sift it through fine muslin, then tie some into a thin muslin, put on the edges of the broken china some white of egg, dust some lime quickly on the same, and unite them exactly.

Ink

To make five gallons of good cheap ink, take half a pound of extract of logwood and dissolve it in five gallons of hot water, and add half an ounce of bichromate potash. Strain and bottle it.

To Improve Pale Black Ink

To a pint of black ink add one drachm of impure carbonate of potassa, and in a few minutes it will be jet black. Be careful that the ink does not run over during the effervescence caused by the potassa.

To Preserve Steel Pens

Metallic pens may be preserved from rusting by throwing into the bottle containing the ink a few nails or broken pieces of steel pens if not varnished. The corrosive action of the acid which the ink contains is expended on the iron so introduced, and will not therefore affect the pen.

Fire Balls For Fuel

Mix one bushel of small coal or sawdust, or both, with two bushels of sand and one bushel and a half of clay, make the mixture into balls with water, and pile them in a dry place to harden them. A fire cannot be lighted with these balls, but when it burns strong put them on above the top bar, and they will keep up a strong heat.

To Purify River or Muddy Water

Dissolve half an ounce of alum in a pint of warm water, and stirring it about in a puncheon of water from the river, all the impurities will soon settle to the bottom, and in a day or two it will become quite clear.

To Give a Cool Taste to Water

A few leaves of sheep mint held in the mouth, or chewed, just before drinking water, will seemingly impart a degree of coolness to the draught.

To Prevent Thirst

Coffee grounds chewed at intervals on a march, or during any arduous service, will repress thirst, and satiate the cravings of hunger. When boiled over again, and the decoction becomes cool, it will quench thirst more effectively than water.

Charcoal Tooth Powder

Pound charcoal as fine as possible in a mortar, or grind it in a mill, then well sift it, and apply a little of it to the teeth about twice a week, and it will not only render them beautifully white, but will also make the breath sweet, and the gums firm and comfortable. If the charcoal is ground in a mortar, it is convenient to grind it in water to prevent the dust from flying about. Indeed the powder is more convenient for use when kept in water.

Wax For Sealing Bottles

Take equal parts of rosin and beeswax and melt over a fire, stir in some Spanish Brown, and while hot dip in the bottles.

Cheap Blacking

To a tea cup of molasses stir in lampblack until it is black, then add the white of two eggs, well beaten, and to this add a pint of vinegar or whiskey, and put it in a bottle for use. Shake it before using.

Chinese Method of Rendering Cloth Waterproof

To one ounce of white wax, melted, add one quart of spirits of turpentine, in which, when thoroughly mixed and cold, dip the cloth and hang up to dry. Try it.

To Clean Kid Gloves

First see that your hands are clean, then put on the gloves and wash them, as though you were washing your hands in a basin of turpentine, then hang them up in a warm place, or where there is a good current of air, which will carry off all smell of turpentine. This method was brought from Paris, and thousands of dollars have been made by it.

To Bleach Straw Hats, &c.

Straw hats and bonnets are bleached by putting them, previously washed in pure water, into a box with burning sulphur, the fumes which arise unite with the water on the bonnets, and the sulphurous acid thus formed bleaches them.

To Remove Grease From Cloth

Take soft soap and fuller's earth, of each half a pound, beat them well together in a mortar, and form cakes. The spot first moistened with water is rubbed with the cake and allowed to dry, when it is well rubbed with a little warm water, and afterwards rinsed or rubbed clean.

To Remove Grease From Books

Lay upon the spot a little magnesia or powdered chalk, and under it the same, set on it a warm flat iron, and as soon as the grease is melted it will all be absorbed, and leave the paper clean.

To Make Old Silk Look as Well as New

Unpick the dress, grate two Irish potatoes into a quart of water, let it stand to settle, strain it without disturbing the sediment and sponge the silk with it. Iron on the wrong side.

Powder to Clean Gold Lace

Rock alum (burnt and finely powdered,) five parts, levigated chalk one part, mix. Apply with a dry brush.

To Keep Arms and Polished Metal From Rust

Dissolve one ounce of camphor in two pounds of hog's lard, observing to take off the scum, then mix as much black lead as will give the mixture an iron color. Fire arms, &c., rubbed over with this mixture, left twenty-four hours, and then dried with a linen cloth, will keep clean for many months.

To Make Economical Wicks For Lamps

When using a lamp with a flat wick, if you take a piece of clean cotton stocking it will answer the purpose as well as the cotton wicks which are sold in the shops.

To Dry Herbs

Dry the gathered crop, thinly spread out and shaded from the sun, tie the herbs in small bundles, and keep them compactly pressed down and covered with white paper; or, after drying them, put each sort into a small box, and by means of boards fitted in it, and a screw-press, press the herbs into cakes or little trusses. These should be afterwards carefully wrapped up in paper and be kept in a dry place, when they will retain their aroma as perfectly as when they were put into the press, for at least three years. By the common method of hanging up herbs in loose bundles the odor soon escapes.

An Illuminated Bottle

By putting a piece of phosphorus the size of a pea into a phial, and adding boiling oil until the bottle is a third full, a luminous bottle is formed, for on taking out the cork to admit atmospheric air, the empty space in the phial will become luminous. Whenever the stopper is taken out at night, sufficient light is evolved to show the hour upon a watch, and if care be taken to keep it generally well closed it will preserve its illuminative power for several months.

A Cheap Taper For a Sick Room

Take a piece of soft pliant paper, part of newspaper for example, and form a circle of it, then gather the centre together and twist it into a wick, immerse the whole in a saucer of lard and light it, and you have a taper that will last some hours.

To Prevent Blisters on the Feet

Blistering or soreness of the feet may be prevented on long marches by covering the soles of the stockings with a coating of the cheapest brown soap. Coarse cotton socks are the best for walking.

Tough Meat

Those whose teeth are not strong enough to masticate hard beef should cut their steaks the day before using into slices about two inches thick, rub over them a small quantity of soda, wash off next morning, cut them into suitable thickness, and cook according to fancy. The same process will answer for any description of tough meat.

Cheap Door Mats

Cut any old woolen articles into long strips, from one to two inches broad. Braid three of these together, and sew the braid in gradually increasing circles till large enough.

Economy in Carpets

In buying a carpet, as in everything else, those of the best quality are cheapest in the end. As it is extremely desirable that they should look as clean as possible, avoid buying a carpet that has any white in it. Even a small portion of white interspersed through the pattern will in a short time give it a dingy appearance. If you cannot obtain a hearth rug that exactly corresponds with the carpet, get one entirely different, for a decided contrast looks better than a bad match.

Various Hints

One flannel petticoat will wear nearly as long as two, if turned behind part before, when the front begins to wear out. If you have a strip of land do not throw away soapsuds. Both ashes and soap suds are good manure for bushes and young plants.

See that nothing is thrown away which might have served to nourish your own family, or a poorer one.

"Brewis" is made of crusts and dry pieces of bread soaked a good while in hot milk, mashed up, and eaten with salt.

Charcoal powder will be found a very good thing to give knives a polish.

A bonnet and trimmings may be worn a much longer time if the dust be brushed well off after walking.

A bowl containing two quarts of water, set in an oven when baking, will prevent pies, cakes, &c., from being scorched.

RECIPES FOR MAKING BREAD, &c., FROM RICE FLOUR

To Make Loaf Rice Bread

Boil a pint of rice soft, add a pint of leaven, then three quarts of rice flour, put it to rise in a tin or earthen vessel until it has raised sufficiently; divide it into three parts, and bake it as other bread, and you will have three large loaves, or scald the flour, and when cold mix half wheat flour or corn meal, raised with leaven in the usual way.

Another

One quart of rice flour, make it into a stiff pap, by wetting with warm water, not so hot as to make it lumpy, when well wet add boiling water, as much as two or three quarts, stir it continually until it boils, put in half pint of yeast when it cools, and a little salt, knead in as much wheat flour as will make it a proper dough for bread, put it to rise, and when risen add a little more wheat flour, let it stand in a warm place half an hour, and bake it. This same mixture only made thinner and baked in rings make excellent muffins.

Johnny or Jonny Cakes

To three spoonfuls of soft boiled rice add a small tea cup of water or milk, then add six spoonfuls of the rice flour, which will make a large Jonny cake or six waffles.

Rice Cakes

Take a pint of soft boiled rice, a half pint of milk or water, to which add twelve spoonfuls of the rice flour, divide it into small cakes, and bake them in a brick oven.

Rice Cakes Like Buckwheat Cakes

Mix one-fourth wheat flour to three-fourths superfine rice flour, and raise it as buckwheat flour, bake it like buckwheat cakes.

To Make Wafer

Take a pint of warm water, a teaspoonful of salt, add a pint of the flour and it will give you two dozen wafers.

To Make Rice Puffs

To a pint of the flour add a teaspoonful of salt, a pint of boiling water, beat up four eggs, stir them well together, put from two to three spoonfuls of lard in a pan, make it boiling hot and fry as you do common fritters.

To Make a Rice Pudding

Take a quart of milk, add a pint of the flour, boil them to a pap, beat up six eggs, to which add six spoonfuls of Havana sugar and a spoonful of butter, which when well beaten together add to the milk and flour, grease the pan it is to be baked in, grate nutmeg over the mixture and bake it.

Rice Flour Sponge Cake

Made like sponge cake, except that you use three-quarters of a pound of rice flour, thirteen eggs, leaving out four whites, and add a little salt.

Rice Flour Blanc Mange

Boil one quart of milk, season it as to your taste with sugar and rose water, take four table-spoonfuls of the rice flour, mix it very smooth with cold milk, add this to the other milk while it is boiling, stirring it well. Let all boil together about fifteen minutes, stirring occasionally, then pour it into moulds and put it by to cool. This is a very favorite article for invalids.

Rice Griddle Cakes

Boil one cup of whole rice quite soft in milk, and

while hot stir in a little wheat flour or rice flour when cold, add two eggs and a little salt, bake in small thin cakes on the griddle.

In every case in making rice flour bread, cake or pudding, a well boiled pap should be first made of all the milk and water and half the flour, and allowed to get perfectly cold before the other ingredients are added. It forms a support for them, and prevents the flour from setting at the bottom, stir the whole a moment before it is set to cook.

HINTS FOR THE LADIES

Some of the more economical readers may be glad to have a little advice as how to freshen up a dress of which they have got tired, or which may be beginning to lose its beauty. Those which are soiled, or worn at the bottom may be made up so as to look very well at very small expense, and with little trouble. Thus, for a dress of fancy material, a band of alpaca between five and six inches in width will suffice to renew it. This band should be waved at the top, and piped with a thick blue or red piping. The sleeves must have a similar reverse, and a little Swiss body, trimmed also with a piping, will complete the costume. For taffetas dresses the band should be of the same material, but black, and finished off at the top in the same manner; or, if a more simple arrangement be preferred, it may be headed with two or three rows of narrow ribbon plated in the middle. A band might be replaced with two flounces, or pinked black taffetas; these will have a better effect if placed a little distance from another, and with a heading.

If it should happen that a skirt of taffetas requires widening, and all thought of matching the dress has been given up, the only resource left is to insert plain bands. If the dress be of a deep shade, we would advise that the bands be made of black taffetas not quite eight inches wide, and put in between each breadth; in this style the skirt will have no trimming at the bottom, unless it be a band of black taffetas in wide scollops or festoons, one scollop reaching just across the breadth of the taffetas from one black band to the next; this should be headed by a narrow ruche of ribbon, and a similar ruche placed up each black band up the skirt. In setting this dress on to the skirt, care should be taken to so arrange the plates that the black band may be folded under so as not to show at the waist. A Swiss sash should be added as a finish to the body, and plain turned-back cuffs. If the dress be a light-colored plain taffetas, the best arrangement will be to make the bands of the same color, but of a deeper shade, and the little ruche should be composed of narrow guipure instead of ribbon. – *Le Follet.*

Made in the USA
Coppell, TX
17 September 2021

62495886R00089